Unterwegs in
Berlin

Unterwegs in

Berlin

Text von Moritz Fahrner
Fotos von Reiner Elsen und andere
Übersetzung von Chris Abbey

ADMOS

Titel:
Die Kuppel des neuen Reichstages nach Plänen des Architekten Norman Foster.

Schloss Charlottenburg.

Internationales Kongresszentrum mit Funkturm.

Eine der acht Skulpturen auf der Schlossbrücke, nach Schinkels Plänen gefertigt.

Frontispiz:
Die Siegessäule am Großen Stern.

Inhaltsverzeichnis:
Der mit der Philharmonie verbundene Kammermusiksaal.

Frontcover:
The dome of the new Reichstag according to the plans
of the architect Norman Foster.

Schloss Charlottenburg.

Internationales Kongresszentrum with Funkturm.

One of the eight sculptures on the Schlossbrücke,
produced according to the plans of the German architect Karl Friedrich Schinkel.

Frontispiece:
The Siegessäule at the traffic intersection known as Großer Stern.

Contents:
The Kammermusiksaal connected with Philharmonie.

© by ADMOS Verlagsaktiengesellschaft, Leipzig und Frankfurt/Main
Mitherausgeber: Berlin Tourismus Marketing GmbH,
Spreequell Mineralbrunnen GmbH

Alle Rechte an Text und Bild vorbehalten.
Nachdruck, auch auszugsweise, nur nach schriftlicher Genehmigung
des Verlages gestattet.
Gestaltung: Matthias Dittmann, Mügeln
Lektorat: Christian Kupfer, Steffi Hohensee
Gesamtherstellung: ADMOS Verlags-AG Leipzig
Printed in Germany 2000
ISBN 3-934042-60-0

Inhalt

Contents

Vorwort

Berlin – die Stadt, in der von nun an Regierung und Parlament arbeiten – hat viele Gesichter: In der Vergangenheit war es die Mauer, dann waren es die Baukräne, die das Bild der Spree-Metropole prägten. Zu Beginn des neuen Jahrtausends ist es vor allem das „Neue Berlin", das mit seinen gerade entstandenen oder kurz vor ihrer Vollendung stehenden Bauten am Potsdamer Platz, am Pariser Platz oder auch im Regierungsviertel für Schlagzeilen sorgt und Gäste aus dem In- und Ausland lockt: Insgesamt 75 Millionen Tagesbesucher und 4,2 Millionen Übernachtungsbesucher entscheiden sich pro Jahr für eine Reise nach Berlin und küren die Metropole an der Spree damit zum beliebtesten Städtereiseziel in Deutschland.

Doch nicht nur seit den neunziger Jahren erfreut sich die Stadt im Herzen Europas bei nationalen und internationalen Besuchern großer Beliebtheit: Berlin war und ist von jeher ein zentraler Ort für Reisende aus aller Welt. Der Potsdamer Platz der 30er Jahre war der verkehrsreichste Platz Europas. Am Ende dieses Jahrhunderts – nach fast drei Jahrzehnten mauerbedingter Verödung – ist dieser Platz gerade im Begriff, neue verkehrstechnische und städtebauliche Visionen für das Berlin des kommenden Jahrtausends zu entwickeln und spiegelt somit den Auf- und Umbruch der gesamten Stadt wider. Ihren besonderen Reiz erfährt die Metropole aus ihrer geographischen Lage, quasi als Ost-West-Schnittstelle eines zusammenwachsenden Europas.

Weltweite traurige Berühmtheit hat die Metropole durch die Berliner Mauer erlangt. Nach dem Wegfall dieses makabren Touristen-Magnets ist Berlin dabei, sein Image neu zu definieren. Das attraktive Reiseziel ist als „Werkstatt der Einheit" für den Besucher aus dem In- und Ausland interessanter denn je. Einige Mauerreste können auch heute – über zehn Jahre nach dem Mauerfall – noch besichtigt werden, z. B. an der East Side Gallery, in der Bernauer Straße, am Preußischen Landtag und am Prenzlauer Berg. Als Kultur-Metropole hat sich die einstige offizielle Kulturstadt Europas weit über ihre Grenzen hinaus einen Namen gemacht. Mit rund 170 verschiedenen Museen und Sammlungen verfügt Berlin über eine vielseitige Museumslandschaft, wie sie kaum eine andere Metropole bieten kann. Neben ihren attraktiven Museen offeriert die Hauptstadt zahlreiche weitere kulturelle Höhepunkte – von den Internationalen Filmfestspielen über die Berliner Philharmoniker bis hin zu hochkarätigen Aufführungen in den mehr als 135 Theatern und Bühnen der Stadt. Berlin ist aber nicht nur für kulturinteressierte Besucher ein wahres Mekka, sondern auch für Erholungssuchende. Die Spree-Metropole ist reich an innerstädtischen Parks wie der Tiergarten, der Botanische Garten und der Zoologische Garten, der der artenreichste und flächenmäßig größte Europas ist. Die zahlreichen Flüsse und Kanäle hingegen können im Sommer mit Fahrgastschiffen befahren werden.

Wir möchten sie sehr herzlich einladen, mit Hilfe dieses Bildbandes Berlin zu entdecken und schätzen zu lernen. Sollten sie nach dem Lesen des Buches neugierig geworden sein auf die Metropole, so würden wir uns sehr freuen, Ihnen bei der Gestaltung Ihres nächsten Berlin-Aufenthaltes (BTM-Informations-Hotline 030/01 90 75 40 40, die Reservierungs-Hotline 030/25 00 25 oder via Internet – www.berlin-tourismus.de) behilflich sein zu können und Sie in Berlin herzlich begrüßen zu dürfen.

Hanns Peter Nerger
Geschäftsführer der Berlin Tourismus Marketing GmbH

Im August 1961 lässt die DDR eine Mauer an der Demarkationslinie zwischen Ost- und Westberlin errichten. Erst im Herbst 1989 wird sie durchlässig durch die revoltierende Bevölkerung der DDR. Gänzlich abgerissen wird die Mauer bis Dezember 1990.

In August 1961, East Germany erected a wall on the demarcation line between East and West Berlin. The Berlin Wall remained unbroken until November 1989, when popular unrest forced the government to open the border. The Berlin Wall was completely demolished in December 1990.

Foreword

Berlin – the city in which the German Government and Parliament are now based – has many countenances. Once this city on the River Spree was indelibly associated with the Berlin Wall; nowadays its image is dominated by construction cranes. At the start of the new millennium, it is above all the 'New Berlin' with its edifices in various stages of completion on Potsdamer Platz, Pariser Platz and the government district which hit the headlines, attracting visitors from Germany and abroad. According to the statistics, Berlin is the most popular destination among the country's cities, with 75 million day trippers and another 4.2 million overnight visitors travelling to the German capital every year.

However, Berlin's popularity didn't just begin in the 1990s. Located at the heart of Europe, Berlin has always exercised a fascination for travellers from all over the world. In the 1930s, Potsdamer Platz was the busiest traffic intersection in Europe. And as the 20th century draws to a close, despite almost three decades of desolation caused by the Wall, this square is currently developing new visions of town and transport planning for the Berlin of the 21st century, epit-

omising the radical changes taking place here. Yet the city's particular appeal stems above all from its geographical position, which makes it the leading East–West interface as Europe converges.

The city rose to notoriety with the construction of the Berlin Wall in 1961. Following the collapse of this macabre tourist magnet, Berlin is now busy redefining its image. Already an attractive destination, the "workshop of unity" is more interesting than ever before for domestic and foreign visitors. Ten years after it was torn down, isolated remains of the Berlin Wall can still be seen, for example at the East Side Gallery, on Bernauer Strasse, at Preussischer Landtag, and in Prenzlauer Berg.

Once the official European cultural capital, Berlin has made a name for itself far beyond its own boundaries as a major arts centre. Containing 170 different museums and collections, Berlin has a unique museum scene which is virtually unparalleled. In addition to attractive museums, the capital also boasts numerous cultural highlights – ranging from the International Film Festival and the Berlin Philharmonic Orchestra to top-class performances in the city's more than 135 theatres. Then again, Berlin is also the place to go for those simply wanting to relax. The numerous rivers and canals can be explored by passenger ship in the summer, while thanks to the city's parks like the Botanical Gardens and its two main zoos, Berlin contains more species of animals and open spaces than any other city in Europe.

We hope that the illustrations in this book will tempt you to discover and savour Berlin. Should be interested in exploring Berlin for yourself, we would be delighted to help you arrange your next stay in this exciting city. Just contact BTM Information-Hotline on + 49 1805 75 40 40 (only for calls from abroad). All visit our home page (www.berlin-tourism.de).

Hanns Peter Nerger
Managing Director of BTM (Berlin Tourismus Marketing GmbH)

Der Zoologische Garten wurde 1844 als erster Zoo in Deutschland auf dem Gelände der Fasanerie eröffnet. Heute besitzt er den größten Tierbestand aller zoologischen Gärten der Welt. Der aufgerichtete Bär ist das Wappentier der Hauptstadt.

The Zoological Garden was opened on the site of the pheasantry in 1884 as the first the zoo in Germany. Nowadays Berlin Zoo has more animals than any other zoo in the world. The rearing bear is the heraldic beast of Berlin.

Ganz Berlin ist eine Wolke

Eine Metropole sucht einen neuen Mythos

Der Besuch der alten Dame findet pünktlich statt. Hedwig Wahle fährt jeden Nachmittag im Taxi beim Hotel Adlon am Pariser Platz vor. Dort wartet schon der Hotelportier mit dem wallenden Mantel, der sie durch die Lobby an ihren Tisch geleitet. Von dort hat sie alles im Blick, vom Pianisten, dem sie so gern zuhört, bis zu den interessanten Leuten, die sich in der Lobby aufhalten, vom Plätscherbrunnen mit den Fröschen bis zum Rezeptionstresen. Die Serviererin bringt ein Kännchen Kaffee und ein Stück Torte. Die alte Dame besitzt mehrere eigene Immobilien, aber diese Immobilie ist ihr die liebste von allen. „Das Adlon ist mein liebster Zeitvertreib", sagt Hedwig Wahle. „Das hat mehr Programme als mein Fernsehapparat."

Am nächsten Tag ist sie wieder da. Der Direktor, der manchmal auf einen Schwatz vorbeikommt, nennt Hedwig Wahle den treuesten Gast des Hauses. Das freut die alte Dame. Warum sie so gern ins Adlon geht? Weil sie nicht mehr geglaubt hat, daß der glanzvolle Hotelpalast, in dem sich vor dem Krieg die Reichen und Schönen versammelten, je wiedererstehen würde. Sie ist eine Urberlinerin, ihr liegt die Stadt am Herzen, „und daß sich so viele Mühe geben, damit sie noch schöner wird", das ist für sie, die bald das zehnte Lebensjahrzehnt erreicht haben wird, eine grandiose Erfahrung.

Berlin, Berlin? Mehr als vier Jahrzehnte in zwei Stadthälften geteilt, die feindlichen ideologischen Lagern zugehörig waren, verlor die Stadt ihren Metropolenstatus. Frontstadt im Westteil, künstliche Hauptstadt im Ostteil. Nun sind die beiden einsamen Inseln wieder zusammengewachsen, die Insulaner sind per demokratischem Dekret zu Hauptstädtern mutiert, die Stadt ist wieder zu einem Knotenpunkt zwischen Ost und West geworden. Das neue Berlin, wie es allenthalben heißt. Berlin, Berlin!

Verglichen mit Rom oder Paris ist Berlin (noch) keine singulär schöne Stadt. Noch gleicht sie vielerorts dem Aschenputtel, das vorgibt, mehr zu sein, als es ist. Berlins Fieberkurve steigt und fällt täglich zwischen Größenwahn und Zerknirschung. Mal ist sie postulierte Hauptstadt der

Berlin is just one big cloud

A metropolis seeks a new myth

Every afternoon, regular as clockwork, Hedwig Wahle alights from her taxi outside Hotel Adlon on Pariser Platz. The hotel porter in his flowing coat is already waiting to escort her through the lobby to her table. From this vantage point, she can see everybody and everything – the pianist whose playing she adores, the interesting people in the lobby, the burbling fountain with the frogs, and the reception desk. The waitress brings her a small pot of coffee and a slice of cake. The elderly lady may own several other properties, but this is clearly her favourite place to be. "The Adlon is my very own old-people's home," says Frau Wahle. "Coming here's a real treat. There's more action here than on my television!"

She's back the next day. The manager, who sometimes stops for a chat, refers to Hedwig Wahle as his most loyal guest, which delights her. Why does she love going to the Adlon so much? It's because she never expected that the glittering hotel palace where the rich and beautiful used to meet before the war would ever be rebuilt. She's a Berliner through and through and deeply attached to the city. Not far off her 90th birthday, she is thrilled that so many people are working hard to make it even more beautiful.

"Berlin, Berlin?" as the song goes. Divided for over four decades between two hostile ideological camps, the city lost its role as a major metropolis. Instead it became West Germany's front-line city, and East Germany's artificial capital. Now these two isolated islands have been reunited. The islanders have metamorphosed by democratic decree into inhabitants of the capital, and the city has regained its former status as the place where East meets West. "This is the new Berlin," is what they're all saying. "Berlin, Berlin!"

Compared with Rome or Paris, Berlin is not an especially beautiful city – at least, not yet. In many places it still rather resembles Cinderella pretending to be more than she actually is. Berlin's temperature chart fluctuates daily between megalomania and remorse. Sometimes it is the self-styled capital of the arts, organising its own leading art exhibitions, and containing more museums than there are rainy days in the year,

Hotel Adlon – ein Hotel der Spitzenklasse am traditionellen Ort in traditioneller Architektur.

Hotel Adlon – a first-class hotel at traditional location in traditional architecture.

Kunst, rüstet kulturell auf mit eigener Biennale, Kunstmessen, mehr Museen als Regentagen und Hunderten interessanten Galerien. Mal gibt sie sich spröde, ist für ihre Bewohner und Besucher nur Standort im nüchtern-prosaischen Sinn und führt einen rauhen, schnippischen Dialekt.

Die Ruppigkeit der Berliner ist von jeher bekannt. „Es sind mehrere Flaschen Poesie nötig, damit man in Berlin etwas anderes sieht als tote Häuser und Berliner", hämte Heinrich Heine 1828. Theodor Fontane meinte, wer ein echter Berliner werden wolle, müsse lernen, einen fremden Menschen auf der Straße anzurempeln mit den Worten: „Pass doch besser uff!" Und Heiner Müller, der große Dramatiker der DDR, der Ost-West-Grenzgänger, pflegte gern zu spotten: „Wenn schon Provinz, dann Berlin."

„Die größte Tugend Berlins war, sich selber immer distanziert und ironisch zu sehen", sagt der Verleger und intime Berlin-Kenner Wolf Jobst Siedler. An dieser Souveränität fehle es noch im neuen Berlin. Aber die Stadt sei wieder auf dem Weg dahin, meint Siedler, weil sie die Chance genutzt habe, mit neuer, mutiger, teils umstrittener Architektur auf sich aufmerksam zu machen, weil sie den traditionsreichen „Laufstraßen" – Unter den Linden vom Brandenburger Tor bis zur Museumsinsel, die Leipziger Straße als

along with hundreds of interesting galleries. Sometimes it radiates aloofness, or is just a place to live and work for its inhabitants, where visitors are met by a rough, cocky dialect.

The Berliners have long been known for their gruffness. "It takes several bottles of poetry before you can see more in Berlin than just dead buildings and Berliners," poet Heinrich Heine remarked spitefully in 1828. Theodor Fontane said that all it takes to become a genuine Berliner is an ability to barge into complete strangers in the street with the words "Look where you're going!" And Heiner Müller, the great East German dramatist and cross-border commuter between the two Germanies, liked to mock, "If it must be the provinces, then Berlin."

"Berlin's biggest virtue was that it always took a reserved, ironic view of itself," according to publisher and Berlin expert Wolf Jobst Siedler. This sovereignty is something the new Berlin has yet to recapture. But it will succeed, believes Siedler – because it has grabbed the opportunity to draw attention to itself with new, courageous and sometimes controversial architecture, because it has recognised the importance of traditional boulevards like Unter den Linden stretching from the Brandenburg Gate to the Museum Island, the shopping street Leipziger Strasse or

Mit dem Bau der Mauer zum Niemandsland degradiert, zeigt sich der Potsdamer Platz heute als größte Baustelle Europas. Wie sich die neue Mitte Berlins in Zukunft darstellen wird, erfährt man in der Infobox am Leipziger Platz.

Degraded into no man's land by the construction of the Berlin Wall, in the mid-1990s Potsdamer Platz suddenly flourished into the largest building site in Europe. The Infobox on Leipziger Platz shows what the future holds in store for the centre of Berlin.

„Kaufstraße" und die Friedrichstraße, einst mit 123 Destillen, Kneipen und Bordellen als „Saufstraße" bezeichnet – wieder den richtigen Platz im Stadtbild zuweise. So schnell wie Berlin in den letzten zehn Jahren gewachsen sei, seien die Berliner und Neu-Berliner nicht mitgewachsen. Vielen ginge es zu schnell mit der neuen Gründerzeit.

Die „angeborene Wurstigkeit" (Fontane) der Berliner hat schon vielen zu schaffen gemacht. Sie ist Notwehr, denn Großstädter müssen mit ganz anderen Zumutungen fertig werden als Zeitgenossen in idyllischeren Regionen. In der Großstadt ballt sich alles, hier finden die Konflikte statt, werden die Zukunftsentwürfe multikulturellen Zusammenlebens vorweggenommen, ist die Sozialisation viel weiter vorangekommen als in Mittel- und erst recht Kleinstädten. Berlin war immer ein Laboratorium der Moderne, und ist es nun erst recht. Lange Zeit ein Biotop im Schatten der Mauer, im Niemandsland zwischen Nato und Warschauer Pakt, bot es einer Fauna und Flora Zuflucht, die anderswo als Ungeziefer und Unkraut bekämpft worden wäre: Künstler, Literaten, Anarchisten, Terroristen, Stasi-Zuträger, Oberbonzen, Hausbesetzer, Wehrdienstverweigerer, Lebenskünstler, Lesben, Schwule, linke Professoren und kommunistische Nationalisten.

that "road of revelry" Friedrichstrasse (once boasting 123 bars, pubs and brothels) and has restored them to their proper place in the city. Berlin may have grown fast over the past 10 years, but Berliners and new Berliners are having a job to keep up with the pace of development. The Berliners' "innate couldn't-care-less attitude" has already been a source of trouble for many. But it's just a way self-defence, because city-dwellers have to cope with much more bother than their contemporaries in more pastoral regions. The city is a melting pot, a venue of conflict. It's where the future multicultural society is happening now, a place where socialisation has advanced much further than in medium-sized or small towns. Berlin has always been a laboratory of the modern age, and never more so than now. For decades a biotope in the shadow of the Berlin Wall, in no man's land between NATO and the Warsaw Pact, it sheltered creatures who elsewhere would have been fought as vermin: artists, writers, anarchists, terrorists, secret police informers, top Communist Party hacks, squatters, conscientious objectors, masters in the art of living, lesbians, gays, left-wing professors and communist nationalists. Berlin was the home of minorities and extremists on both sides of the Wall. No other city in Germany or

*Tiergarten. Gläserne Kuppel
im Reichstagsgebäude.*

*Tiergarten. The glass dome
on the Reichstag building.*

11

Berlin war auf beiden Seiten des Todesstreifens die Heimat von Minderheiten und Extremisten. Keine andere Stadt in Deutschland, ja, in Europa, hat so viel Toleranz gewagt. Berlin ist ein Sonderfall in nahezu jeder Hinsicht. Die einzige deutsche Stadt, die Deutschen und ausländischen Besuchern eine ganz eigene Wahrnehmung der deutschen Wirklichkeit ermöglichte. Wenn das keine Leistung ist.

Das Ertragen von Dissonanzen hat an der Spree Tradition. „Berlin schafft es, die Nachteile einer amerikanischen Großstadt mit denen einer deutschen Provinzstadt zu verbinden", schrieb Kurt Tucholsky in den zwanziger Jahren des 20. Jahrhunderts. Nun aber ist Berlin wieder Hauptstadt, Repräsentationsort der Deutschen, sucht die Metropole einen neuen Mythos.

Das heißt: Schwerstarbeit. Denn Berlin hatte nie, wie andere Städte ihrer Größe und Bedeutung, Zeit, Patina anzusetzen und einen eigenen Charme zu entwickeln. Berlin war immer etwas, aber dieses Etwas nur für – historisch gesehen – kurze Zeit. Mal Preußenresidenz mit asketischem Pomp, mal wilhelminischer Militärstandort mit Großmachtambitionen, mal Vorreiter der Industriellen Revolution, mal das Germania der Hitlerei, mal die Hauptstadt des roten Bonzenstaates und Europas größte Subventionsinsel. Rasanz ist das Merkmal dieser Stadt, heute dies und morgen das. Ewige Verlässlichkeiten gab es nie. Das hat dazu geführt, daß Berlin nicht in Würde und Erstarrung vor der eigenen Schönheit altern konnte. Berlin ist eine unfertige Stadt, ewig jung, stets im Wandel, nie in ergebener Ruhe wie etwa Paris in seinem konstanten Glanz.

Die alte Dame hat es instinktiv erfasst. Adlon verpflichtet und hilft weiter im Selbstverständigungsprozess beider gegensätzlicher Stadthälften. Die Rekonstruktion des Hotelbaus fand im ehemaligen Osten an der Grenze zum ehemaligen Westen statt – an traditioneller Stelle. Ein besonderer, exemplarischer Ort von großer symbolischer Kraft. Da lässt es sich nicht nur gut Kaffee trinken, sondern auch vorzüglich nachdenken über den Zeitenlauf. Berlin ist die aufregendste Stadt Deutschlands, hier geschieht alles im Voraus, alles konzentriert. Die Ost-West-Stadt, traditionell eine Drehscheibe von Menschen und Mentalitäten, eignet sich wie keine andere Stadt, Europa zu wagen.

Ganz Berlin ist eine Wolke. Staub, Bauschutt und damit einhergehende Verkehrsänderungen machen es den Berlinern nicht leicht. Aber der Umbau wird vollendet werden, das Bild der Zukunft gewinnt jeden Tag mehr an Schärfe. Berlin hat es wieder einmal geschafft.

anywhere else in Europe dared to be so tolerant. Berlin is a special case in almost every respect. It was the only German city which granted Germans and foreigners alike a unique perception of German reality. No mean achievement. Tolerating dissonance goes back a long way in Berlin, a city which (wrote Kurt Tucholsky in the 1920s) "... managed to combine the disadvantages of an American city with those of a German provincial town." Yet now Berlin has become the capital again. Fronting the German people, the metropolis is now seeking a new own myth.

It's not an easy task. Unlike other cities with a similar size or rank, Berlin never had the time to take on a hallowed air of tradition and develop its own charm. Berlin has always been something special – but never for very long. Once the Prussian capital residence with ascetic pomp, then Kaiser Wilhelm's headquarters with great ambitions of power, once the forerunner of the industrial revolution, then Germania of the Hitler era; and then the capital city of a Red state headed by the chosen few, and Europe's largest subsidised island. Speed is the distinguishing feature of this city; today this, tomorrow that. Nothing has ever afforded eternal reliability, and so Berlin has never had the chance to age with dignity, ossified by its own beauty. Berlin is an unfinished city, eternally young, constantly changing, never resting in resigned calm in its immutable splendour like, say, Paris.

And this is something the old lady has grasped instinctively. The Adlon has obliged by helping the two opposing halves of the city come to terms with one another. The hotel was rebuilt on what used to be the border between East and West Berlin, and what is nowadays known as central Berlin. This is a special area of great symbolic power. A great place for not only a cup of coffee, but also for contemplating the course of history. Berlin is the most exciting city in Germany, everything is concentrated here, everything here happens ahead of time. This East–West city, always a crossroads of people and mentalities and never more so than today, is the most suitable place for tackling the new Europe. Berlin has put the past behind it, and has everything to look forward to. Out of the dust of history and the mud of the building sites, a new metropolis is emerging. Berlin is one big cloud. Dust, building rubble, the resulting traffic chaos and other changes means it's not easy living in Berlin. But one day reconstruction will be over, and the image of the future is growing sharper with every passing day. Once again, Berlin has made it.

Tiergarten. Das Reichstagsgebäude wurde 1884–94 gebaut. Nach umfangreichen Aus -und Umbauten in den Jahren 1995–99 nach Plänen des britischen Architekten Norman Foster ist der Reichstag Tagungsort des Bundestages.

Tiergarten. The Reichstag building was built between 1884–94. Following extensive alteration in 1995–99 directed by British architect Norman Foster, the Reichstag is the home of the Bundestag, the German parliament.

Seiten 14/15
Vor dem Alten Museum, das 1824–28 von Karl Friedrich Schinkel erbaut wurde, entstand eine nach holländischem Vorbild gestaltete Gartenanlage, der Lustgarten.

A Dutch-style pleasance was laid out in front of the Altes Museum, which was built by Karl Friedrich Schinkel in 1824–28.

Charlottenburg. Das Theater des Westens, in den Jahren 1895/96 von Bernhard Sehring errichtet, gilt als die einzige Berliner Bühne, die sich ausschließlich der Pflege des Musicals verschrieben hat.

Charlottenburg. Erected in 1895/96 by Bernhard Sehring, Theater des Westens is the only Berlin theatre exclusively devoted to musicals.

Der Travestie-Künstler Romy Haag.

Travesty artiste Romy Haag.

Das Pergamonmuseum ist das jüngste, größte und bedeutendste Gebäude auf der Museumsinsel. Es ist benannt nach dem berühmten, nach Zeus und Athene geweihten Altar, der in der Antike zu den sieben Weltwundern gehörte. Das Museum gelangte zu seinem Weltruhm durch die beispielhafte Präsentation antiker Monumentalarchitektur: Pergamon-Altar, Markttor von Milet und Ischtar-Tor von Babylon.

The Pergamon Museum is the youngest, largest and most prestigious building on Museum Island. It was named after the famous altar consecrated in Pergamon by Zeus and Athena, which in classical antiquity was one of the seven wonders of the world. The museum came to prominence due to its exemplary presentation of antique monumental architecture: the Pergamon Altar, the market gate of Miletus, and the Ishtar Gate of Babylon.

Rund um Preußens Gloria

Nirgendwo ist Berlin so geschichtsträchtig wie auf der Straße Unter den Linden

„Unter den Linden bin ich immer gerne gegangen. Am liebsten, du weißt es, allein", schreibt Christa Wolf in einer Erzählung. Das ist nach wie vor ein guter Tipp. Wer hier gesammelt entlangschlendert, wird auf der 1,5 Kilometer langen und 60 Meter breiten Straße auf jedem Meter die Repräsentation Berlins erleben. 1647 war die Straße auf Anordnung des Kurfürsten Friedrich Wilhelm angelegt worden. Auf den 250 „Rheinländischen Routen", wie das Maß damals hieß, entstand eine Galerie aus sechs Reihen Linden- und Nussbäumen, später nur Lindenbäumen. Entscheidend geprägt aber wurde die Allee, wie so vieles in Berlin, zur Zeit Friedrichs des Großen, der in den Jahren zwischen 1771 und 1776 für ein völlig neues Aussehen von Berlins Vorzeigestraße sorgte.

44 alte Wohnhäuser werden abgebrochen, 33 neue entstehen. Zu Ehren des großen Preußenkönigs wird nach dessen Ableben ein Denkmal in Auftrag gegeben, das, von Christian Daniel Rauch geschaffen, auf der Mittelpromenade aufgestellt wird.

Der preußische Corso, der den Krieg zwar schwer beschädigt, aber mit dem Großteil seiner Substanz überstanden hat, reihte eine klassische Architektur an die andere und war einst höherwertig als die Pariser Champs-Élysées aus dem Kaiserreich Napoleons oder Roms Via Veneto mit ihren Bürgerpalästen aus dem Fin de siécle. Der Zeitenlauf machte vieles davon zunichte. Immerhin blieben ganze Bauten aus Berlins klassischer Epoche wie aufgereiht erhalten. Sie bieten die Chance, auch optisch an Vergangenes anzuknüpfen, an die Zeit, als Berlin unbestritten eine der stilbildenden Weltstädte war.

Die Allee kann wieder mit sich selbst imponieren, sie ist ein Corso zum Sehen und Gesehenwerden, für die Berliner untereinander und für ihre Besucher. Dennoch ist der Wiederaufbau der „Linden" nicht nur das Präparieren einer Bühne, auf der ein altes Stück stattfinden soll. Dieser Straße kommt eine bestimmte Aufgabe im Stadtzusammenhang zu: Sie verkörpert das Alte und das Neue zugleich. Sie schafft Identität, weil sie Tradition verkörpert, peilt aber auch in

Prussia's glory

Nowhere in Berlin is as steeped in history as Unter den Linden

"I've always enjoyed strolling beneath the lindens – especially on my own, as you know," writes Christa Wolf in one of her stories. And it's still a good idea. Those who take a relaxed walk along this boulevard measuring a mile long and over 60 yards wide experience the prestige emanated by Berlin at every step.

The street was laid out in 1647 on the order of Elector Friedrich Wilhelm. On an area measuring 250 "Rhineland routes", a gallery of six rows of linden and walnut trees was planted, although later only linden trees stood there. Yet like much of Berlin, the avenue's appearance was largely moulded under Frederick the Great, who ordered a facelift for Berlin's eminent boulevard between 1771 and 1776. Forty-four old dwelling houses were demolished and 33 new ones built. Following Frederick's death, Christian Daniel was commissioned to construct a monument in his honour on the central promenade.

Prussia's very own Via del Corso, which largely survived the war despite being severely damaged in parts, contains one classical building after the other. With its palatial *fin-de-siècle* town houses, it once ranked more highly that the Parisian Champs Élysées in Napoleon's empire or Rome's Via Veneto. Although many of these buildings were scarred by the passage of time, a number of complete buildings from Berlin's classical era have still been preserved. They provide an optical link with the past – with a time when Berlin was undisputedly one of the trend-setting cities of the world.

The avenue is once again a stirring place to see and be seen – for both Berliners and their guests. Yet the reconstruction of the avenue means far more than just preparing a stage for an old play. This boulevard has a certain function in the city. It simultaneously embodies the old and the new. Creating identity by virtue of its history, it also looks ahead to the future as its gaps are filled with new designs.

In the 19th century, avenues became the leading street type employed in modern cities. In Europe they were used to break up the medieval districts full of twisting backstreets and to adapt towns to

Erlebnis

Unter den Linden
Brandenburger Tor,
Pariser Platz,
Lindencorso,
Staatsbibliothek,
Humboldt-Universität,
Königliche Bibliothek,
Staatsoper,
Kronprinzenpalais,
Schinkelsche Neue Wache,
Zeughaus
Schlossplatz/Lustgarten,
Dom,
Schinkelsche Schlossbrücke

Attractions

Unter den Linden
Brandenburg Gate,
Pariser Platz, Lindencorso,
State Library, Humboldt
University, Royal Library,
State Opera House,
Opera Palace,
Crown Prince's Palace,
Schinkel's New Guardhouse,
Armoury,
Schlossplatz/ Lustgarten,
Cathedral, Schinkel's
Schlossbrücke (bridge).

Das Denkmal Friedrich des Großen, die Neue Wache und das Zeughaus bilden auf der 1500 m langen und 60 m breiten Straße Unter den Linden ein bemerkenswertes Ensemble.

The statue of Frederick the Great, Neue Wache and Zeughaus form a remarkable ensemble on the 1500m-long and 60m-wide "Unter den Linden" boulevard.

19

Das Hauptgebäude des Brandenburger Tores wird von einem Vierspänner, der 1794 nach Plänen von Johann Gottfried Schadow erstellten Quadriga gekrönt.

The main building of the Brandenburg Gate is crowned by the Quadriga – a chariot drawn by four horses driven by Victoria wearing a laurel wreath, which was designed by Johann Gottfried Schadow and built in 1794.

die Zukunft, denn sie wird in ihren Lücken aufgefüllt, gestaltet.

Alleen avancierten im 19. Jahrhundert zur wichtigsten Straßenform moderner Großstädte, mit ihnen wurden in Europa die mittelalterlich verwinkelten Städte aufgebrochen und den neuen Verhältnissen angepasst. Die breite, von hohen Fassaden gesäumte und von Alleebäumen bestandene Stadt-Traverse realisierte und multiplizierte das moderne Leben in seiner Vielfalt. Sie war die konsequente Ausdrucksform einer neuen Vitalität, wie sie mit der Neuzeit über die großen Städte des Kontinents kam. Ursprünglich gedacht als Ausfallstraße für die kurfürstlichen Jagden, wurde die „Linden" aber bald zum Lieblingsplatz von Stadtplanern und Architekten. Schlüters Zeughaus war das Modell, an dem sich die künftigen Bauwerke dieser Straße orientierten. Das Zeughaus wurde selbst maßstäblich für das Schloss, beeinflusste das nobel unterkühlte Rokoko Knobelsdorffs und sämtliche Bauten Schinkels, des größten Architekten Preußens, dem Meister des preußischen Klassizismus. Um 1800 sind alle wichtigen Fassaden fertig, 1810 eröffnet die Universität in einem ehemaligen Palais, treten aber auch die leichten Damen im

the new conditions. The broad thoroughfare lined by tall buildings and trees reflected and multiplied modern life in all its diversity. It was the logical expression of a new vitality flowing out of continental cities in the modern era. Originally planned as a main road leading out of the city for Electoral hunts, the "Linden" soon became the favourite place of town planners and architects. Schlüter's Armoury was the model on which the future buildings of this street were based. The Armoury even served as a model for the palace, influenced the noble, dry rococo created by Knobelsdorff and all the buildings erected by Schinkel, Prussia's greatest architect and master of Prussian classicism. All the major facades had been completed by around 1800, in 1810 the university opened in a former palace – and it was also at this time that the loose-living ladies from Madame Charlotte Schuwitz's establishment appeared. The avenue suddenly became a marshalling route for soldiers and *flâneurs*, businessmen and idlers, diplomats, comedians and women of easy virtue. Prussia's main street was lined by the city palaces of the Prussian nobility and the smart set of Berlin. The "Linden" became the city's stage and the grandstand of the

20

Etablissement der Madame Charlotte Schuwitz in Erscheinung. Die Allee ist auf einmal Verschiebestrecke für Soldaten und Flaneure, Geschäftsleute und Müßiggänger, Diplomaten, Komödianten und Frauen mit lockeren Sitten. Gesäumt ist die Hauptstraße Preußens von den Stadtpalästen des preußischen Adels und der Berliner Schickeria. Die „Linden" sind zur Bühne der Metropole geworden und zur Tribüne des Königreiches Preußen. Deutlich zum Ausdruck kommt das am Brandenburger Tor, von Langhans im Stil der Propyläen errichtet, mit der von Gottfried Schadow entworfenen Siegesgöttin Viktoria im Wagen mit vier Rössern. Die fünf Meter hohe Quadriga, 1794 vollendet, wurde zum prachtvollen Abschluss des Boulevards. Zur DDR-Zeit entfernte man auf Geheiß Ulbrichts den preußischen Adler und das Eiserne Kreuz; nach der Rekonstruktion 1991 wurden sie wieder eingesetzt. Dass der Verkehr heute wieder durch das Brandenburger Tor fließt, gibt dieses Wahrzeichen der Bevölkerung zurück; 1791 war es für Durchfahrten geöffnet worden. Auf dieser Straße ist er nun wieder zu sichten, der Homo sapiens Germanicus capitalensis, der Hauptstädter. Am liebsten scheint er sich am sonnenbeschienenen Sonntagvormittag auf dem Mittelstreifen aufzuhalten. Da treten die preußischen Pastellfarben der historischen Gebäude ebenso effektvoll wie die neuzeitlichen Bauten und die Bäume, die der Straße ihren Namen gaben, ins Licht.

Die „Linden"-Straße ist oft missbraucht worden, war Paradestrecke der preußischen Soldaten, des wilhelminischen Militärs, reichsdeutscher Ruhmes- und Triumphweg und Aufmarschstrecke von Nationalsozialisten und der Nationalen Volksarmee der DDR (die bizarrerweise den preußischen Stechschritt bevorzugte). Aber hier rollten auch die Kaleschen der lebenslustigen Berliner, die Allee war Zentrum zivilen Lebens im alten Berlin. Am meisten aber war sie der Platz für Preußens Gloria. Museen, Staatsoper und Staatsbibliothek, Humboldt-Universität und Schinkels Neue Wache waren Foren der Monarchie, die es nach glanzvollen Auftritten gelüstete; später auch der Diktaturen und Republiken.

Als Heinrich Heine als Korrespondent für den Rheinisch-Westfälischen Anzeiger in Berlin weilt, fasziniert ihn die Straße zwischen dem Brandenburger Tor und dem Schloss. „Ja, das sind die berühmten Linden, wovon Sie soviel gehört haben", kommt er seinen Lesern ungewohnt persönlich. „Mich durchschaudert's, wenn ich denke: Auf dieser Stelle hat vielleicht Lessing gestanden, unter diesen Bäumen war der

kingdom of Prussia. This role was underlined by the Brandenburg Gate built by Langhans, which was erected after the model of the Propylaea and capped by Victoria (the goddess of victory) in a chariot drawn by four horses. Measuring over five yards tall and completed in 1794, the quadriga formed the magnificent conclusion to the boulevard.

In the East German era, the Prussian eagle and the Iron Cross were removed at Ulbricht's behest, only to be restored in 1991 after the reconstruction of the Brandenburg Gate. The fact that traffic has been allowed to pass beneath the Brandenburg Gate since German reunification symbolises its return to the people; after all, it was originally opened to through traffic immediately after completion in 1791.

Another tradition has been revived with the return of the species *Homo sapiens Germanicus capitalensis* to this avenue. The central strip seems to be his favourite place on a sunny Sunday morning. The Prussian pastel colours of the historical buildings have a similarly dramatic effect to the modern buildings and the trees which gave the street its name.

"Linden" Street has often been misused – as a parade route for Prussian soldiers and Kaiser Wilhelm's armed forces, as a route of glory and triumph in the Third Reich, and as the scene of many a march-past by the East German National People's Army of the GDR (who curiously adopted the Prussian goose-step). But it was also a boulevard along which the barouches of merry Berliners rolled, and the centre of civil life in the old Berlin. Yet most of all it was the home of Prussia's Gloria. Museums, the State Opera and Library, Humboldt University and Schinkel's New Guardhouse were forums of first the monarchy (who yearned for glamorous appearances) and later of dictatorships and republics.

When Heinrich Heine worked as a correspondent for the *Rheinisch-Westfälischer Anzeiger* in Berlin, he was fascinated by this road stretching between the Brandenburg Gate and the palace. "Yes, here are the famous linden you have already heard so much about," he tells his readers in an unusually personal tone. "I tremble to think that Lessing may have stood here, that beneath these trees was the favourite spot for a walk among many a great man who lived in Berlin, and that even the great Fritz himself strolled here! But isn't the present wonderful, too? It is precisely noon, the time when human beauty is out for a walk. The spruce crowd is parading up and down past the lindens. Can you see the elegant man over there with twelve colourful waistcoats? And

Erlebnis

Bauhaus-Archiv,
Klingelhöferstraße 14,
Tiergarten
Arbeiten aus allen Bereichen des ehemaligen Bauhauses Weimar-Dessau-Berlin

Deutsche Staatsoper
(1743)

Haus am Checkpoint Charlie (Mauermuseum),
Friedrichstraße 43/44,
Kreuzberg
Dokumentation des Lebens und Sterbens an der Mauer

Pergamon-Museum,
Museumsinsel, Mitte
Attraktion ist der rekonstruierte Altar von Pergamon

Attractions

Bauhaus Archive,
Klingelhöferstrasse 14,
Tiergarten
Examples of all the areas of work tackled by the former Bauhaus in Weimar, Dessau and Berlin.

German State Opera
(1743).

House at Checkpoint Charlie (museum dedicated to the Berlin Wall),
Friedrichstrasse, Kreuzberg
Documentation on the rise and fall of the Berlin Wall.

Pergamon Museum,
Museum Island, central Berlin
The main attraction is the reconstructed altar by Pergamon.

*Eine Sightseeing-Tour durch
Berlin ist nicht nur für die
zahllosen Touristen interessant.*

*A sightseeing tour of Berlin is
interesting not only for countless tourists.*

Lieblingsspaziergang so vieler großer Männer, die in Berlin gelebt; hier ging der große Fritz, hier wandelte - Er! Aber ist die Gegenwart nicht auch herrlich? Es ist just zwölf und die Spazierenszeit der schönen Welt. Die geputzte Menge treibt sich die Linden auf und ab. Sehen Sie dort den Elegant mit zwölf bunten Westen? Aber schauen Sie die schönen Damen! Welche Gestalten! Ich werde poetisch! Ja, Freund, hier unter den Linden/Kannst du dein Herz erbaun,/Hier kannst du beisammen finden/Die allerschönsten Frau'n."

Das Berliner Volk eignete sich die Straße an, und das war das Beste, was ihr widerfahren konnte. Es gibt Cafés, Konditoreien, Weinstuben. Dann kommt das Adlon, das Bristol, eine immer perfektere Stadtmöblierung. Bereits 1826 flimmert die erste Gasbeleuchtung, 1846 ziehen zwei Pferde den ersten Linienbus durch die Avenue. Im 20. Jahrhundert wird das Ensemble fortwährend komplettiert. Geschäfte und edle Speisetempel laden zum Eintritt - da ist die Straße bereits Touristenadresse. Besucher lustwandeln auf ihr, fahren nach Hause zurück, nach Westfalen, Sachsen oder ins Ruhrgebiet und verkünden stolz: „Berlin jewesen – Kaiser jesehen!" Natürlich Unter den Linden.

In den zwanziger Jahren des 20. Jahrhunderts wird die Straße zum Vorzeigeort einer hektischen Metropole. Walter Mehring dichtet: „Die Linden lang! Galopp! Galopp! Zu Fuß, zu Pferd, zu zweit! Mit der Uhr in der Hand, mit'm Hut auf'm Kopp. Keine Zeit, keine Zeit, keine Zeit!" 1926 residieren Unter den Linden 18 Autosalons, 19 Reisebüros, 17 Juweliere und Bijouterien, 15 Mode-, 13 Zigarren- und sechs Kunstläden. Dazu Banken, Hotels, Büros. Und überall die frechen Berlinerinnen, die nichts anderes im Sinn haben, als Diplomaten, Ministern, Bankiers, Fabrikanten, Anwälten, Künstlern und Journalisten den Kopf zu verdrehen.

Nach dem Auftrieb der Lustbarkeiten die Fakkeln der Nazis. Nach dem Krieg die Aufräumkommandos der FDJ. Das Schloss, noch nahezu intakt, wird gesprengt. Dem würdevollen Architekturzug von neuem Prinzessinnen- und Kronprinzenpalais, Kommode, Zeughaus, Hedwigskathedrale und Staatsoper werden Stilbrüche zugefügt. Der hässliche Bau des Außenministeriums entsteht (inzwischen abgerissen), das Hotel Unter den Linden wird zum Kreuzungspunkt von Botschaftern und Ideologien. Der Kalte Krieg tut der Straße nicht gut, sie wird kujoniert durch architektonischen Mischmasch, und jeden Mittwoch trumpft die sogenannte Arbeiter-und-Bauern-Republik säbelrasselnd und stiefelknallend mit Tschingdarassabum zum Großen

look at the pretty ladies! What figures! I'm getting poetic! Yes, my friend, it's certainly an uplifting experience under the lindens – it's the place where you can meet the world's most beautiful women."

The people of Berlin made the street their own, and this was the best thing which could ever have happened to it. It contained cafés, cake shops and wine bars. Then there were hotels like the Adlon and the Bristol, and ever more refined conveniences – like the first gas lighting in 1826, and the first regular (horse-drawn) bus service along the avenue in 1846. The architectural ensemble was continuously augmented throughout the 20th century. The establishment of shops and top-class restaurants symbolised the arrival of Unter den Linden as a tourist attraction. Visitors took a stroll here and returned home to the German provinces, proudly declaring: "Been to Berlin – seen the Emperor!" And of course Unter den Linden – that went without saying.

In the 1920s, the street became the pride of place of a frenetic capital. Walter Mehring wrote: "Along Unter den Linden at full gallop! By foot, by horse, the two of us! With your watch in your hand and your hat on your head. There's no time to spare, no time to spare!" In 1926 Unter den Linden contained 18 car show rooms, 19 travel agencies, 17 jeweller's shops, 15 boutiques, 13 tobacconists and six art shops, along with a host of banks, hotels and offices. And the avenue was full of those saucy Berlin women whose sole purpose seemed to be to turn the heads of diplomats, ministers, bankers and lawyers.

But this merry scene gave way to the Nazis' torches, and later, after the war, the clearing teams of the Free German Youth organisation. The Palace had remained almost unscathed, yet was blown up. The dignified architectural parade comprising the new Princesses' and Crown Prince's Palaces, the Royal Library, the Armoury, St. Hedwig's Cathedral and the State Opera House became disrupted by ill-fitting intrusions. The ugly building of the Foreign Ministry was erected (only to be demolished following unification), and Hotel Unter den Linden became a meeting place for ambassadors and ideologies.

Wachaufzug auf. Der Westbesuch staunt und zittert vor soviel martialischer Zur-Schaustellung. Nach der Wende Ratlosigkeit. Geliebt wird die „Linden" nicht, es lockt der Parvenü Kurfürstendamm. Doch allmählich wird die Promenade wiederentdeckt. Nobelgeschäfte siedeln sich an, die Kassenhalle der Filiale der Deutschen Bank wird in den Zustand von 1901 zurückversetzt. Die Wirtschaft kommt mit Showrooms und Edel-Fresskneipen, um damit unter Beweis zu stellen, dass auch sie an die Perspektive der Straße glaubt.

Zur Jahrtausendwende Gründerzeitfieber zwischen Pariser Platz und ehemaligem Palast der Republik. Der wieder aufstrebende Prachtboulevard wird zur Bankenmeile. Das bedeutet: Mörtel wird angerührt, Marmor angeliefert, Mosaik gelegt. Die Befürchtung, daß die Aufreihung von Banken die Allee steril machen könnte, hat sich nicht bewahrheitet. Fast alle Geldpaläste sind Vorzeigestücke alter und neuer Architektur. Es ist eine Lust, durch so manche dieser Kassenhallen zu schlendern.

Stück für Stück wird die Promenade umgestaltet. Und die Menschen sind wieder da. „Unter'n Linden, unter'n Linden, gehn spazieren die Mägdelein", heißt es in einer Operette. Es ist die Luft der Bäume, es sind Schaulust und Koketterie, die diese älteste Straße Berlins wieder zu einer ihrer beliebtesten gemacht haben.

The Cold War did not benefit Unter den Linden. The avenue was harassed by architectural hotchpotch, and every Wednesday the Republic of Workers and Farmers put on its changing of the guard to the sound of rattling sabres and thundering boots. Visitors from West Germany trembled in the face of this martial display.

As East Germany crumbled, Unter den Linden was abandoned in favour of the parvenu Kurfürstendamm. Yet gradually the promenade was rediscovered. Classy boutiques opened, and Deutsche Bank's branch here was restored to its 1901 glory. Showrooms and smart restaurants appeared, underlining economic faith in the street's future.

And as the new millennium approaches, the area between Pariser Platz and the disused Palace of the Republic is blossoming into a banking street. It's a hive of activity, with mortar being mixed, marble delivered, mosaics laid. Initial fears that too many banks would make the avenue sterile have proved unfounded. The banks are nearly all gems of architecture old and modern, and some of the banking halls are a feast for the eyes.

Bit by bit, the promenade is being redeveloped. And the people have returned. "The maidens are strolling beneath the lindens," runs the old operetta. The air of the trees, curiosity and coquetry have all combined to make this, Berlin's oldest street, one of its most popular again.

Die Vorzeigeallee Unter den Linden ist vorzüglich für eine Freiluftgaststätte geeignet. Das Café Einstein bietet seinen Gästen einen erfrischenden Ruhepunkt inmitten der Metropole Berlin.

Berlin's showpiece avenue, Unter den Linden, makes an ideal alfresco restaurant. Café Einstein is a welcome oasis amidst this bustling city.

23

Acht Skulpturen aus weißen Carrara-Mamor aus den Jahren 1847–1857 zieren die Schloss-brücke.

Eight sculptures of white Carrara marble from the years 1847 to 1857 adorn the Schlossbrücke.

Neben dem Kronprinzenpalais Unter den Linden steht das Denkmal des Staatsmannes und preußischen Reformers Freiherr vom Stein.

Next to the Kronprinzenpalais ('Crown Prince's Palace') on Unter den Linden stands the monument to the statesman and Prussian reformer Baron vom Stein.

Kaiser Wilhelm II erhielt 1891 den Neptunbrunnen zur Verschönerung des Schlossplatzes geschenkt.

Kaiser Wilhelm II received the Neptunbrunnen in 1891 as a present to embellish the palace square.

Die Humboldt-Universität wurde 1748–53 von Johann Boumann d. Ä. für Prinz Heinrich errichtet.

Humboldt University was set up in 1748–53 by Johann Boumann the Elder for Prince Heinrich.

Die dreibogige Schlossbrücke über einen Spreearm am östlichen Ausgang der „Linden" ist mit überlebensgroßen Mamorfiguren geschmückt.

Schlossbrücke, a triple-arched bridge spanning an arm of the River Spree at the eastern end of Unter den Linden, is decorated with larger-than-life marble statues.

Wie aus dem Ei gepellt

Berlins neue Baugebiete sind Themenparks für Stadtliebhaber

Im 20. Jahrhundert wurde Berlin zweimal Opfer von Zerstörungen. Krieg und Nachkriegszeit setzten der Stadt zu, danach regierten in beiden Stadthälften Mangelplanung und Abrissbirne. Traditionsreiche Orte, wie der Potsdamer Platz, wurden zum Niemandsland der Leere. Der brachiale Mauerbau, auch mitten durch die Innenstadt hindurch, nahm Berlin mit seiner Vergangenheit auch seine Würde. Ab den sechziger Jahren erfolgte der getrennte Aufbau in Ost und West. Die Stadt, die mehr als 700 Jahre eng zusammengewachsen war, verlor ihr Inneres, zerfiel auch optisch in zwei Hälften. Nach den weitgehend missglückten Experimenten des Wieder- und Neuaufbaus in der schwierigen Nachkriegsmoderne geht es nun um das Zurückholen der Innenstadt, um das neue Erbauen einer alten Stadt. Der Potsdamer Platz ist die Probe aufs Exempel, er wird für Berlin bald das sein, was der Eiffelturm für Paris ist. Unter Federführung des Genueser Architekten Renzo Piano ist ein Zentrum im Zentrum entstanden, das in einer Art Generalstabsplan komplett geplant und als schlüsselfertige Paketlösung übergeben wurde. Mit der „Daimler City" ist der größte Teil des Potsdamer Platzes, der schon verloren war, in die Hauptstadt integriert worden. Mit seinem alten Herzen und einem neuen Gesicht ist Berlin wieder Weltstadt und Metropole und erscheint wie aus dem Ei gepellt.

Das Stadtquartier aus der Retorte entstand auf dem Reißbrett und wurde in nur vier Jahren Bauzeit umgesetzt. Gewöhnlich braucht ein solches Wachstum Jahrhunderte. Doch das Brachland zwischen Ost und West gab dem Komplett-Neubau eine Chance. Vom legendären Potsdamer Platz, der schon im 19. Jahrhundert ein belebter und lärmender Verkehrsknotenpunkt war, mit Geschäften und über hundert Restaurants, blieb nur das Weinhaus Huth.

Auch das andere Teilstück, das Sony-Center, ist bereits fertiggestellt. Die Architektur präsentiert sich hier mit großer Geste. Sämtliche Fassaden sind in Ziegelstein, Keramik oder Terrakotta gekleidet, nur warme Erdfarben ließ der Bebauungsplan zu, und alle Gebäude haben

Dressed up to the nines

Berlin's new construction zones – theme parks for city-lovers

Berlin twice became the victim of destruction in the 20th century. The city was plagued by war and the postwar era, and afterwards both halves of the city were dominated by flawed planning and the ball and chain of the demolition teams. Historical sites like Potsdamer Platz became no man's land. The brutal construction of the Berlin Wall ripping right through the centre of the city robbed Berlin of both its past and its dignity, launching the separate development of East and West Berlin in the 1960s. The city which had grown together for over 700 years lost its heart and was divided into two halves with differing appearance.

Following the largely unsuccessful experiments of redevelopment and new construction during the difficult phase of postwar modernism, the goal now is to recover the city centre, to revive the old Berlin. Potsdamer Platz is putting this aim to the test, and will soon become for Berlin what the Eiffel Tower is for Paris. Under the supervision of Genoese architect Renzo Piano, a centre inside a centre was drawn onto the map and then turned into reality in the form of a turnkey project. The completion of Daimler City marks the reintegration of the largest section of the once lost Potsdamer Platz into the capital. The other main part, the Sony Centre, will also be completed soon. With its old heart and a new countenance, Berlin has regained its position as a cosmopolitan city and is dressed up to the nines.

This test-tube district was hatched on the drawing board and built in just four years. Growth on this scale normally takes centuries. Yet the wasteland between East and West provided an unmissable opportunity for a brand-new construction venture. All that has remained of the legendary Potsdamer Platz, which back in the 19th century was a lively intersection containing shops and over a hundred restaurants, is Huth's wine bar.

The architecture on Potsdamer Platz presents itself with a bold flourish. All the facades have been clad in brick, ceramics or terracotta. The development plans only allow warm earth colours, and all the buildings have classical arcades or

Erlebnis

Potsdamer Platz
Vor dem Krieg verkehrsreichster Platz Europas. Nach dem Krieg Brache und Grenzgebiet. Nach der Wende von mehreren Konzernen bebaut

70 Hektar Fläche, von Daimler-Chrysler, Asea Brown Boveri, Hertie und Sony mit 19 Gebäuden bebaut. 500 000 Büro-Quadratmeter, Arkaden mit über 100 Läden und 30 Restaurants, Europas größte Spielbank

Attractions

Potsdamer Platz
Europe's busiest square until World War II, and then wasteland on the frontier zone between East and West Berlin after the war. Scene of intense building development by a number of corporations after German unification.

Measuring over 170 acres, 19 buildings have since been erected by Daimler-Chrysler, Asea Brown Boverie, Hertie and Sony. Office space (550,000 square yards), arcades containing over 100 shops and 30 restaurants, Europe's largest casino.

Die Friedrichstadt-Passagen – Quartier 206. Der von Henry Cobb entworfene Bau imponiert mit seinen zahlreichen Risaliten und Zurückstaffelungen.

Friedrichstadt Arcades – Area 206. The building designed by Henry Cobb with its numerous projections and stepped elements is especially impressive.

29

weitgehend öffentliche Sockelzonen oder klassische Arkaden. Einige der Bürobauten, etwa der Atriumsbau der Debis-Zentrale, gehören zum Elegantesten, was die Büroarchitektur hervorgebracht hat. Über den Büro- und Einkaufshäusern inszeniert sich eine Penthouse-Dachlandschaft mit umlaufender Freilicht-Joggingbahn mit Stadtüberblick direkt an der Traufkante.

Die Türme der Stararchitekten aus aller Welt führen zu vertikaler Verdichtung. Mit freigestellten Terrassenhäusern, Rundtürmen und Flugdächern wurden auch ungewöhnliche Blocklösungen umgesetzt. Die Kompaktheit von Plätzen, Kreuzungen und Straßenräumen, der Abwechslungsreichtum an Höfen, Durchgängen und Blickbeziehungen haben zur Entstehung metropolitaner Schluchten geführt, wie wir sie aus Städten wie New York, Mailand oder Budapest kennen. Aber nicht das amerikanische Stadtmodell der Hochhausagglomeration, sondern die Vorstellung von der kompakten, räumlich komplexen, europäischen Stadt war Grundlage des Entwurfs. Städtisches Leben sollte sich nicht im Innern großstrukturierter Gebäudekomplexe entfalten, sondern auf Straßen und Plätzen. Musicalhaus, Varieté, Casino, Kinos und andere Vergnügungseinrichtungen, Gastronomie und fliegende Händler simulieren die Lebendigkeit des alten Potsdamer Platzes. Dabei ist der Potsdamer Platz nicht nur „ein rund um die Uhr belebter urbanistischer Märchengarten für Erwachsene" (M. Mönninger). Neben Ladenstraßen und Freizeit-Themenparks gibt es auch die stadtverträgliche Mischung aus Wohn- und Gewerbeflächen, die dafür sorgt, dass sich reale Menschen einer realen Arbeitswelt mit Touristen, Shoppern und Leuten, die zahlreiche Entertainment-Angebote – von Dauerausstellungen über Verbrauchermessen bis zur Vielzahl kultureller Offerten – wahrnehmen, auf natürliche Weise kreuzen. Das bedeutet: Der neue Potsdamer Platz ist kein Disneyland für Gaffer und Staunende. Hier wird auch gelebt und gearbeitet, und das ist eine Reverenz an die Qualität des alten Potsdamer Platzes. Urbanität, Lebendigkeit und Vielfalt sind die Qualitäten des neuen Stadtraumes.

Acht Milliarden Mark wurden von Daimler, Sony & Co. investiert, um auf 100 000 Quadratmetern eine neue Stadt in der Stadt entstehen zu lassen. Sie ist zur Jobmaschine geworden, rund 17 000 Menschen haben in Berlins neuer Mitte einen Arbeitsplatz gefunden. Sie haben Büros und Läden bezogen, servieren in gastronomischen Betrieben oder sind in anderen Service-Einrichtungen beschäftigt. Der Handel hat den Potsdamer Platz auf Anhieb angenommen, das

Das Grand Hyatt Hotel am Potsdamer Platz.

The Grand Hyatt Hotel on Potsdamer Platz.

other ground-floor areas largely open to the public. Some of the office buildings, such as the Atrium and Debis's headquarters, are among the most elegant examples of office architecture ever created. The office blocks and shopping centres are capped by a penthouse roof landscape, complete with an open-air jogging track affording a view of the capital.

Towers built by star architects from all over the world have brought about vertical intensification. Unusual block solutions have been implemented using terraced houses and rotundas. The compact nature of the squares, junctions and road areas, and the wealth of variety in the courtyards, passageways and sight-lines have brought about metropolitan ravines reminiscent of those found in cities like New York, Milan and Budapest. However, the design is based not on the American urban model of skyscraper agglomeration, but rather the idea of the compact, spatially complex European city. The idea was to see urban life unfurl not inside large-structured building complexes, but instead on roads and squares. Musical and variety theatre, casinos, cinemas and other places of entertainment, bars and restaurants, and street-traders simulate the liveliness of the original Potsdamer Platz. Yet Potsdamer Platz is not just an "urban adult fairytale glen working round the clock" (M. Mönninger). In addition to shopping streets and theme parks, it also contains a sustainable blend of housing and business premises, making sure that real people encounter a real, functioning world complete with tourists, shoppers and visitors taking in the numerous entertainment facilities from the permanent exhibitions and consumer trade shows to various cultural attractions. The new Potsdamer Platz is no Disneyland for those wide-eyed with amazement. Real people live and work here – a fact which pays homage to the quality of the old Potsdamer Platz. Urbanity, liveliness and variety are the qualities of this new urban district.

Daimler, Sony and all the others have invested a total of DM 8 billion to create a new city within

Who is Who der Einzelhändler listet alle arrivierten Adressen auf. Mit seinen drei Universitäten, 14 Hoch- und Fachschulen sowie knapp 140 000 Studenten besitzt der Wissenschaftsstandort Berlin einen hochkarätigen Nachwuchspool von Absolventen, von denen einige in den Konzernzentralen zum Zuge kommen werden. Der neue Potsdamer Platz sendet mithin auch in psychologischer Hinsicht positive Signale in die Hauptstadt aus.

„Die Rekonstruktion und Umwandlung Berlins in eine Stadt des 21. Jahrhunderts ist das ehrgeizigste architektonische und urbanistische Projekt aller Zeiten – mindestens seit dem Bau der Pyramiden", staunt der peruanische Schriftsteller Mario Vargas Llosa. „Der Science-fiction-Eindruck verstärkte sich abends, wenn die riesigen Baukräne und Silhouetten der Arbeiter sich unter den potenten Scheinwerfern bewegten und an die Dekorationen und Komparsen einer großen Hollywood-Produktion erinnerten."

Mit dem Fall der Mauer wurde in Berlins Mitte eine solch gewaltige Brache zur Neugestaltung freigegeben, wie es das noch nirgendwo in der Welt gab. Riesige Flächen waren von heute auf morgen der Vorstellungskraft und Macht von Politikern, Investoren und Architekten überlassen, hauptsächlich die innerstädtischen Plätze, wie der Leipziger Platz und der Potsdamer Platz, aber auch Kernstücke wie das Spreebogen-Areal am Reichstag und Teile der Friedrichstraße. Die internationale Kritik bestätigt dem Berliner Baumarkt, die richtigen ästhetischen Entscheidungen getroffen zu haben. Die Wiedergewinnung der historischen Dimension des Städtischen scheint in Berlin zu gelingen. Begrüßt wird vor allem, dass nicht in Tabula-rasa-Aktionen die Stadt neu „erfunden" wurde, sondern das Programm „Kritische Rekonstruktion" heißt, dass ganz unterschiedliche Konzepte zum Zuge kamen mit kontrastreichem, belebendem Nebeneinander unterschiedlicher Bauauffassungen. Berlin ist zum Mekka der modernen Architektur geworden, in dem die rationalen Entwurfsmethoden kühner Ingenieure ebenso Heimrecht haben wie die Planungsphantasien der Künstler. Die Neubebauung Berlins fundiert auf der Tradition des abendländischen Urbanitätsbegriffs und vollendet sich als vitale, moderne Großstadt mit allen dazugehörigen funktionalen wie strukturellen Potentialen. Die städtebauliche Vielfalt des alten Berlin wird im neuen Berlin fortgeschrieben. Liegt die Geschichte des Stadtaufrisses unter der neuen Gebäudemasse auch buchstäblich begraben, ist der künftige Umbau der Metropole Berlin doch von historischen Vorgaben inspiriert.

a city on an area measuring nearly 25 acres. It has become a veritable job machine, providing work for some 17,000 people. They have moved into offices and shops, or are working in cafés and restaurants or other service establishments. Shopping took off immediately at Potsdamer Platz, and the list of retail outlets reads like a Who's Who of famous names. With its three universities, 14 colleges and nearly 140,000 students, Berlin is a centre of learning possessing a first-class pool of graduates, some of whom will one day be in the boardrooms of top corporations. Hence it should not be overlooked that the new Potsdamer Platz is also transmitting positive psychological signals into the new capital.

"The reconstruction and transformation of Berlin into a 21st-century city is the most ambitious architectural and urbanistic project ever — at least since the construction of the pyramids," says Peruvian author Mario Vargas Llosa in wonder. "The science-fiction impression was amplified in the evenings, when the enormous cranes and the silhouettes of the building workers moved about beneath the powerful floodlights, looking like the scenery and extras on a gigantic Hollywood set."

The fall of the Berlin Wall meant that a huge amount of wasteland suddenly became available overnight for redevelopment in the heart of the city on a scale previously unheard of. Vast areas — primarily the inner-city squares, but also core areas such as the Spreebogen district near the Reichstag and parts of Friedrichstrasse — were left to the imagination and power of politicians, investors and architects. International assessment has confirmed that the construction market made the right aesthetic decisions in Berlin, where the historical dimension of urban life appears to have been recovered. Particular approval has been voiced concerning the fact that instead of reinventing the city in a clean sweep, the course has been one of "critical reconstruction", allowing completely different concepts and the lively juxtaposition of contrasting architectural approaches. Berlin has become a Mecca of modern architecture which is home to both the rational designs of bold architects and artists' planning fantasies. The new construction of Berlin is based on the traditional Western concept of urbanity, and it is evolving into a vital, modern city with all the necessary functional and structural potential. The urban diversity of the old Berlin is being continued in the new. The historical development of the city's layout may have been literally buried beneath the massive new buildings — yet transformation has truly been inspired by historical guidelines.

Erlebnis

Areal Spreebogen
Kanzleramt und Parlamentsneubauten, Paul-Löbe-Haus und Marie-Elisabeth-Lüders-Haus

Lehrter Bahnhof
Zentralbahnhof in Moabit Zwei ICE-Strecken werden unterirdisch herangeführt und kreuzen sich nördlich des Spreebogens

Friedrichstadt-Passagen I
Das Quartier 206 ist ein heller Komplex mit gefalteten Fassaden

Friedrichstadt-Passagen II
Das Quartier 207 bezieht u.a. das Kaufhaus Galeries Lafayette ein

Friedrichstadt-Passagen III
Das Quartier 205 ist ein ausgedehntes Büro-, Wohn- und Geschäftshaus aus zwei Längs- und drei Quertrakten sowie sechs Vorbauten mit Dachterrassen

Attractions

Spreebogen district
Chancellor's office and new parliamentary buildings – Paul Löbe House and Marie Elisabeth Lüder House.

Lehrter Bahnhof
Central railway station in Moabit – underground intersection of two InterCity routes north of Spreebogen.

Friedrichstadt Arcades I
Area 206 is a bright complex containing entwined arcades.

Friedrichstadt Arcades II
Area 207 includes the department store Galeries Lafayettes.

Friedrichstadt Arcades III
Area 205 is an extended block containing shops, housing and offices comprising longitudinal sections crossed by three perpendicular sections, as well as foreparts with roof terraces.

Im Oktober 1998 wurde nach nur vierjähriger Bauzeit
das Daimler-Chrysler-Areal am Potsdamer Platz eingeweiht.

In October 1998, after a construction period lasting just
four years, the Daimler-Chrysler Area on Potsdamer Platz
was officially opened.

Der Potsdamer Platz. Das Hotel Esplanade, der U-Bahnhof
und das Weinhaus Huth sind die einzigen Bauwerke, die die
Kriegszeit in der ursprünglichen Form überstanden haben.

Potsdamer Platz. Hotel Esplanade, the underground station
and Huth's wine bar were the only buildings to survive the
war in their original form.

Von besonderer Bedeutung
für die Hauptstadtplanung ist
der Spreebogen am nördlichen
Rand des Tiergartens.

The island Spreebogen, located
at the northern edge of the
Tiergarten, is of particular
importance for the planning of
the capital city.

Moderne Kunst vor dem
Debis-Bürohaus am Potsdamer
Platz.

Modern art in front of the
Debis office block on the
Potsdamer Platz.

Innerhalb des Daimler-Chrysler-Areals befinden sich die überdachten Potsdamer-Platz-Arkaden.

The roofed Potsdamer Platz Arcades are located within the Daimler-Chrysler Area.

Friedrichstadt-Passagen. Jean Nouvels Block (Quartier 207) der Galerie Lafayette.

Friedrichstadt Arcades Jean Nouvel's block (Area 207) for Galeries Lafayette.

Die Stadt der Kieze

Berlins Stadtbezirke – Treibhäuser verschiedenster Lebensgefühle

„Der Berliner hat keine Zeit", schrieb Kurt Tucholsky. „Der Berliner ist meist aus Posen oder Breslau und hat keine Zeit. Er hat immer etwas vor, er telefoniert und verabredet sich, kommt abgehetzt zu einer Verabredung und etwas zu spät – und hat sehr viel zu tun. In dieser Stadt wird nicht gearbeitet – hier wird geschuftet."

Was der Satiriker anklingen ließ, trifft auch heute noch zu: Der Berliner ist – öfters, als man glaubt – ein Zugereister. Aus Schlesien allerdings kommt er nicht mehr, dafür aber aus der ganzen Welt. Die Stadt ist wieder der Schmelztiegel, der sie schon einmal war, bevor der Faschismus Hunderttausende in die Emigration nötigte. Es ist eine der großen Traditionen dieser Stadt, dass sie schon sehr früh und beispielhaft vorführte, dass und wie multikulturelles Nebeneinander funktioniert. „Ich weiß nicht, wie viele Lateinamerikaner es in Berlin gibt, aber es müssen viele Hunderte sein, vielleicht Tausende, und ich bin sicher, dass es jeden Tag mehr werden, weil die Hauptstadt Deutschlands sich in einen Magneten für die ganze Welt verwandelt hat... die Stadt ist zu einer gigantischen Metropole geworden, die einen Prozess radikaler gesellschaftlicher Umwandlungen durchmacht", schreibt Perus Nationaldichter Mario Vargas Llosa. Man habe „das prickelnde Gefühl, sich im Zentrum des Universums zu befinden... Berlin wird in den kommenden Jahren Paris als intellektuelle Hauptstadt Europas ablösen. Berlin wird ohne Zweifel eher europäisch als preußisch, kosmopolitisch, multikulturell und demokratisch sein."

Hauptstadteuphorie und Umbau kaschieren nur schlecht, dass Berlin eine Ansammlung von Dörfern ist, jeder Bezirk mit eigenem Geschäfts- und Verwaltungszentrum, mit Rathaus und Markt, Kino und Stadtbibliothek, Schwimmbad und Sportplatz. Und das, obwohl Berlin alles hat, was es zu einer würdevollen Kapitale macht: große Verkehrsachsen, stolze Boulevards, traditionsreiche Plätze und großräumige städtische Erholungslandschaften sowie eine ländliche Idylle als Umgebung, mit am Ende der Eiszeit entstandenen Seen, mit Kiefernwäldern im Urstromtal der Spree, mit Bauernhöfen und

A mosaic of neighbourhoods

Berlin's districts – hothouses of life and living

"Berliners never have any time," wrote Kurt Tucholsky. "The Berliner usually comes from Poznan or Wrocław, and is always busy. He's always got something planned, is always on the telephone making appointments, always turning up late to meetings in a dreadful rush – and he's always very busy. In this city people don't work – they toil."

More than sixty years after his death, Tucholsky's description of Berliners remains as true as it ever was. Berliners tend to be newcomers more than one might expect. But instead of coming mainly from Silesia, nowadays they come from all over the world. Berlin has once again become the melting pot which it was before fascism forced people to emigrate in their hundreds of thousands. Long before anywhere else, Berlin showed the world just how a multicultural city can function. "I don't know how many Latin Americans there are in Berlin, but there must be several hundred or perhaps even thousands, and I'm sure that there are more everyday, because Germany's capital has been turned into a magnet for the whole world – the city has become one gigantic metropolis, which is undergoing a process of radical social transformation," writes Peruvian author Mario Vargas Llosa. You have "the thrilling feeling of being at the centre of the universe.... In the coming years Berlin will replace Paris as the intellectual capital of Europe. There's no doubt that Berlin will become cosmopolitan, multicultural and democratic, and more European than Prussian."

Reconstruction and euphoria at being the German capital fail to conceal the fact that Berlin is a collection of villages, that each district has its own business and administrative centre, its own town hall and marketplace, cinemas and municipal library, swimming pool and sports ground. And this is true despite Berlin having everything it needs to make it a dignified capital: large transport axes, proud boulevards, historical squares and spacious public recreation areas, as well as peaceful countryside nearby, including lakes formed at the end of the ice age, and pine forests in the Spree valley complete with farms and beer

Köpenick. Orgelricke und der Hauptmann von Köpenick: zwei Berliner Originale.

Köpenick. Orgelricke and the Captain of Köpenick are two Berlin originals.

Prenzlauer Berg

In der Rykestraße gibt es eine als Hinterhaus gebaute Synagoge zu besichtigen (nur am Samstag, Sabbat)

Jüdischer Friedhof nördlich des Senefelder Platzes, 1827 angelegt

Der Wasserturm stammt von 1875 und ist heute mit Wohnungen bestückt, ringsherum ist das Zentrum des Szenelebens Prater mit Gartenareal, kleiner Bühne und großem Festsaal in der Kastanienallee 7-9

Schönhauser-Allee-Arkaden mit Einkaufs- und Vergnügungspassagen

Jede Woche wird im statistischen Mittel ein Café, eine Kneipe oder ein Restaurant geöffnet

Eckkneipen, Künstlerateliers, Musikklubs, kleine Gewerbebetriebe, Tante-Emma-Läden

Attractions

Prenzlauer Berg

Rykestrasse contains a unique synagogue erected in a tenement house courtyard (only open on the Sabbath).

Jewish Cemetery north of Senefelder Platz, laid out in 1827.

The water-tower was built in 1875 and has since been converted into housing, while the surrounding area is regarded as the 'scene centre'.

Prater with garden – small stage and large banqueting hall at Kastanienallee 7–9.

Schönhauser Allee Arcades, containing shopping and entertainment arcades.

In statistical terms, a new cafe, pub or restaurant is opened on average once a week.

Corner pubs, artists' studios, music clubs, small businesses, corner shops.

Gartenlokalen. Aber den Berliner, der das alles für sich reklamiert, gibt es nicht. Der Berliner ist Zehlendorfer oder Marzahner, Kreuzberger oder Pankower. Ihn interessiert zuallererst und zuallerletzt, was dort passiert, in seinem Kiez, und zeigt nur selten großstädtisches Profil, etwa wenn es um Hertha BSC geht, Berlins Fußballmannschaft mit Bundesliga-Format.

Der Prenzlauer Berg wird immer noch in Reiseführern als typischer Berliner Kiez vorgestellt. Aber das geschlossenste Gründerzeitviertel Europas, zugleich eines der größten Sanierungsgebiete des Kontinents, mit alten Kneipen und „hipper" Szene, mit Omas, die am Kollwitzplatz wie eh und je ihre Kissen auf die Fensterbretter legen und kunstsinnig abgedrehtem Jungvolk, ist inzwischen Berlins wichtigster Transitbezirk. Innerhalb von fünf Jahren hat sich die Bevölkerung zur Hälfte ausgetauscht, großteils durch Zuzug. Der „Prenzlberg" ist zum Markenartikel geworden und firmiert unter dem Label „nicht normiertes Leben". Zu seinem Logo gehören abblätternde Fassaden, ramponierte Bürgersteige und das Klischee vom Wilden Osten. Anarchische Hinterhöfe, Brandmauern mit rauher Malerei und Heerscharen alternativ gekleideter und so agierender Mitmenschen schaffen eine Atmosphäre, die auf viele anziehend wirkt. Es ist die Dialektik von Boheme und Konsum, Widerständigkeit und Aussteigertum, die das Interesse weckt. Obwohl die Künstler, die den Prenzlauer Berg berühmt gemacht haben, nie mehr als ein Prozent der dortigen Bevölkerung ausmachten. Die Szene, die zu DDR-Zeiten in einer Grauzone siedelte, ist nach der Wende schick und international geworden. Zwischen das Sargmagazin, die Molkerei Marx und die Bäckerei drängen sich heute elsässische und arabische Gastronomen, irische Pubs und kubanische Rum-Bars. Die touristische Kolonisierung des Viertels hat nicht die Anwohner verdrängt. Der „Prenzlberg" ist vorwiegend ein Milieu alter und junger Leute, Familien ist es hier zu wenig Grün und Licht. Beide kommen fast durchweg glänzend miteinander aus, das Motto heißt leben und leben lassen. Das Szenelokal öffnet seine Tür gleich neben dem Altentreff, den es schon zur DDR-Zeit gab. Der Prenzlauer Berg ist nicht ein typischer Berliner Stadtbezirk, gehört aber zu den originellsten Kiezen der Stadt.

Das Wort Kiez stammt aus dem Slawischen, bezeichnete ursprünglich eine Fischersiedlung, später ein geschlossenes Viertel und meint heute ein Quartier mit besonderer Kultur. Aus dem Kiez erwächst das „Milljöh", entspringen Gestalten wie Franz Biberkopf, der Hauptmann von Köpenick oder Liebling Kreuzberg.

gardens. Yet Berliners never claim all Berlin for themselves. Berliners are proud of coming from Zehlendorf or Marzahn, Kreuzberg or Pankow. They are chiefly interested in what's happening in their own *Kiez* or neighbourhood, and only rarely adopt an all-Berlin mantle when talk turns to, say, Hertha BSC, Berlin's first-division football team.

Prenzlauer Berg is still described in the guidebooks as a typical Berlin *Kiez*. Yet this most built-up *fin-de-siècle* district in Europe (and now also one of the largest redevelopment areas on the continent) with its old pubs and hip scene, where old women still place their cushions on the windowsill and watch the world go by on Kollwitzplatz, and with its younger, artistically minded inhabitants, has since become Berlin's leading transit district. Within five years, half the population has been replaced, largely by new arrivals. "Prenzelberg" has become a brand name for the out-of-the-ordinary living. Its logo includes peeling facades, battered pavements and all the clichés of the Wild East. Anarchic backyards, firewalls with rough painting, and hordes of humans alternatively dressed and acting accordingly create an atmosphere which many find appealing. It is the dialectics of Bohemianism and consumerism, resistance and dropping out, which is so fascinating. Even so, the artists who made Prenzlauer Berg famous never accounted for more than one per cent of the local population. The scene which in East German times populated a grey area has since become chic and international. Now jostling for position between the coffin shop, Marx's dairy and the baker's are Alsatian and Arab restaurants, Irish pubs, and Cuban rum bars. Yet the locals have not been driven out, despite the colonisation of the district by tourists. Containing too little greenery or light for families, "Prenzelberg" is mainly a place for young and old. And both generations get along famously: "live and let live" is the district's motto. Alternative clubs are right next door to day-centres for the elderly set up before unification. Prenzlauer Berg may not be typical of Berlin, but it's certainly one of the city's most original *Kieze*.

The word *Kiez* is of Slavic origin, and originally meant a fishing settlement. Later it was used to describe a built-up area, and nowadays it refers to an area with a special culture. From the *Kiez* emerges the milieu, spawning such characters as Franz Biberkopf from Alexander Square, and the Captain of Köpenick. The *Kiez* is a village in the city, a place where everything is close by, whose inhabitants are united by the local diet of beer, rissoles and blustering. But another typical

Erlebnis

Kulturbrauerei e.V. an der Schönhauser Allee, Ecke Knaackstraße, riesiges Karree in neogotischer Ziegelsteinbauweise mit vier Innenhöfen, 1891 für Schultheiß als größte Brauerei Europas eingeweiht, heute multifunktionales Kultur- und Veranstaltungszentrum mit der Sammlung für Industrie- und Alltagskultur der DDR

Event

Kulturbrauerei on Schönhauser Allee (junction with Knaackstrasse) – huge neo-Gothic brickwork construction with four court-yards, built in 1891 by Schultheiss as the largest brewery in Europe, now a multifunctional arts and events centre featuring an exhibition on East German industrial and everyday culture.

Der Kiez ist ein Dorf in der Stadt, ein Ort der kurzen Wege, dessen Bewohner Schwadronieren, Biertrinken und Bulettenessen vereint. Aber es ist auch immer die ganz besondere Biotop-Atmosphäre, die typisch ist für diese besondere urbane Kultur.

Da ist zum Beispiel der Beusselkiez, ein Gründerzeitviertel in der nordwestlichen Ecke des Bezirks Tiergarten. Er entstand als Arbeiterquartier in den Gründerjahren, als die Gutsbesitzerfamilie Beussel auf ihren Moabiter Ackerflächen um 1880 Industrieanlagen und um sie herum Häuser für die Arbeiter errichten ließ. Heute liegt hier vieles im Argen, obwohl noch ein Großteil des gründerzeitlichen Wohnungsbestands vorhanden ist. Der Beusselkiez, nur fünf Autominuten vom Regierungsviertel entfernt, versucht nun sein Schmuddelimage loszuwerden und sich im Wettbewerb der Stadtbezirke neu zu positionieren. Die Einwohner selbst forcieren die Stadtteilsanierung, wollen ihre Eckkneipen gegen die Konkurrenz von Spielhallen halten und freuen sich darüber, dass die meisten Lebensmittelläden nicht großen Supermarktketten gehören, sondern Leuten aus dem Kiez, davon mehr als ein Drittel Ausländer. Sie drängen darauf, dass trotz der Sanierung das Wohnen im Kiez für Ansässige erschwinglich bleiben muss und der kleinbürgerliche Charakter des Viertels erhalten bleibt. Der einstige Arbeiterkiez soll zum Dienstleisterkiez, die traditionelle Mischung aber erhalten werden.

aspect of this special urban culture is its distinct biotope atmosphere.

A good example is "Beusselkiez", a late-19th-century district in the north-western part of Tiergarten, which arose when the Beussels, a family of landowners, built industrial plants on their farmland in Moabit in around 1880 and surrounded them with housing for the workers. Nowadays much of the area is in a sorry state, even though the majority of the housing stock still stands. Situated just five minutes away by car from the government district, Beusselkiez is now trying to shed its grubby image and reposition itself in the ranking of Berlin districts. The inhabitants themselves are taking an active interest in local redevelopment. They want to preserve their traditional corner pubs in the face of competition from amusement arcades, and are pleased that most of the food shops in the area do not belong to any of the large supermarket chains but instead to local people (a third of all grocers being foreigners). The inhabitants insist that housing remain affordable for the population despite refurbishment, and that the lower middle class character of the district be retained. The former workers' neighbourhood is now set to become a service neighbourhood, with the traditional mix still being maintained.

Berlin is a jigsaw puzzle of worlds populated by the lower middle-class which contribute much more to Berlin's image that the newly built districts. The corner pub, a Berlin institution,

Tiergarten. Im Zentrum des 1920 geschaffenen Verwaltungsbezirkes liegt der gleichnamige Park. Ursprünglich kurfürstliches Jagdgebiet, wurde er ein Eldorado für Erholungsuchende.

Tiergarten. At the centre of this administrative district established in 1920 is Tiergarten Park. Originally a royal hunting ground, it has since become an eldorado for those seeking relaxation.

Zu den sehenswerten historischen gastronomischen Ein-
richtungen gehört der Gasthof
„Alter Fritz" in der Karolinen-
straße in Tegel. Das Bier kommt
aus der hauseigenen Brauerei.

Alter Fritz on Karolinenstrasse
in Tegel is one of the finest-
looking historical restaurants
and brews its own beer.

Berlin ist ein Puzzle solcher Kleinbürgerwelten.
Sie prägen die Stadt mehr als die neuen Areale.
Die Eckkneipe, eine Berliner Institution, gehört
als Biotop des Nachbarschaftsgefühls dazu. Dort
verschließt sich die Stadt gegen ihre riesige
Ausdehnung, macht sich aber auch in der Klein-
gruppe mit dem neuen Metropolenstatus ver-
traut. Die Kiezkultur beruht auf Solidarität und
ist mit den aufgesperrten Blechmäulern der
Müllcontainer, den dunkel gestrichenen Woh-
nungstüren und den Zeichen des Verfalls vorder-
gründig hässlich. Aber sie verkörpert ein Lebens-
gefühl, Gemeinschaft, Verlässlichkeit.

„Never leaving the Kiez", hieß die Cartoon-Serie
einer Chicagoer Künstlerin, die einige Zeit im
Prenzlauer Berg lebte. Als Zugereiste erkannte sie
schnell, dass auch Berliner, wie alle Großstädter
der Welt, zuerst Bewohner ihres Viertels sind.
Auch ein anderer Zugewanderter, ein chinesi-
scher Maler, seit vielen Jahren in Berlin, brachte
es auf den Punkt, indem er mit dem Lächeln des
Buddhas sagte: „Ick bin ein Prenzlberger."

In Berlin leben beinah eine halbe Million
Ausländer, die aus 180 Ländern stammen. Die

functions as a biotope of neighbourhood feeling.
This is where the city shuts itself off from its
enormous expansion, yet where small groups get
to grips with Berlin's new capital status. The Kiez
culture is based on solidarity, and is superficially
ugly with its gaping rubbish bins, dark doors
and signs of decay. But they embody an aware-
ness of life, a feeling of community spirit, and a
sense of dependability. "Never leaving the Kiez"
was the title of a series of cartoons by a Chicago
artist who had spent some time in Prenzlauer
Berg. Being a newcomer, she quickly realised
that Berliners (like the inhabitants of capital
cities all over the world) are first and foremost
inhabitants of their respective districts. Another
immigrant, a Chinese painter who has been in
Berlin for several years, hit the nail on the head
by saying with a smile of which Buddha would
be proud, "I come from Prenzelberg."

Half a million foreigners from 180 countries
live in Berlin. Only a very few of them came
as refugees. Most arrived in Germany as students, trainees, migrant workers, or simply as
globe-trotters. The largest minority in the capital

wenigsten landeten als Flüchtlinge hier, die meisten kamen als Studenten, Auszubildende, Arbeiter, Weltreisende. Die größte Minderheit der Hauptstadt sind die 140 000 Türken; sechs von zehn Berliner Türken sind hier geboren. Kreuzberg ist ihr traditionelles Revier, es ist ein bisschen wie Klein-Istanbul. Die Türken haben ihre eigenen Märkte und Geschäfte (und dort sehr viele Berliner als Kunden), ihre Moscheen und andere Treffpunkte, ihre Restaurants und natürlich, wie in jeder Großstadt, auch ihre eigene Mafia. Sie picknicken an warmen Tagen im Görlitzer Park und hupen fröhlich in den Straßen herum, wenn sie Braut und Bräutigam im Mercedes zum Standesamt kutschieren.

Auch die Russen, traditionell in Berlin zu Hause, sind wieder da. Ihre Zahl wird auf 120 000 Personen geschätzt, darunter viele Juden, die den Status von Kontingentflüchtlingen haben. Es gibt kyrillischsprachige Zeitungen, russische Teestuben, in denen der Samowar blubbert, ein russisches Radio- und Fernsehprogramm und Konzerte Berliner Orchester, in denen russische Musiker dominieren. Die Russen waren schon zu Beginn des 20. Jahrhunderts in Berlin beheimatet, die revolutionären Wirren brachten fast die gesamte geistige Elite von St. Petersburg und Moskau an die Spree. Seither gehört die russische Kultur zu Berlin.

Am eindrucksvollsten ist aber die jüdische Wiedergeburt des Scheunenviertels in den letzten Jahren, des östlichen Teils der Spandauer Vorstadt. 1866 öffnete hier die erste Synagoge ihre Pforten, der prunkvolle Kuppelbau, trotzig den beiden anderen Kuppeln von Stadtschloss und Dom beigesellt, wurde zum Wegweiser für viele von Pogromen und Armut vertriebenen ostjüdischen Zuwanderern aus der Ukraine, Galizien und Russland.

Diese Kultur, durch den Holocaust nahezu ausgelöscht, kehrt allmählich in ihr angestammtes Quartier zurück. Es gibt wieder ein jüdisches Gymnasium, koschere Restaurants, eine junge, bunte und quirlige Szene, die aus den Nachfahren derer besteht, die dem Genozid ausgeliefert waren. Die jüdische Wiedergeburt des Scheunenviertels hat etwas Unverhofftes, beinahe Märchenhaftes. So wie die wiederhergestellte, glanzvolle goldene Kuppel der Neuen Synagoge. Berlin hat ein neu heranwachsendes Hauptzentrum, ist jedoch geprägt von seinen vielen Nebenzentren in den Bezirken. Das hat mit historischen Reminiszenzen zu tun, macht die Gebrauchsanweisung für die Hauptstadt nicht einfach, verleiht ihr aber auch folkloristisches Flair mit den „Treibhäusern" unterschiedlicher Lebensgefühle.

comprises the 140,000 Turks, and 60% of Berlin's Turks are born here. Kreuzberg is their traditional preserve, and it has something of the air of Little Istanbul. The Turks have their own markets and shops (serving many Berliners), their own mosques and other meeting places, restaurants and, of course, like in every city, their own mafia as well. On hot days they picnic in Görlitz Part and toot away on their car horns whenever they escort a Mercedes taking a couple to the registry office.

The Russians, who traditionally have always been at home in Berlin, have returned again too. Their number is put at 120,000, and they include many Jews, who have the status of contingent refugees. There are newspapers using the Cyrillic alphabet, Russian tea-rooms with samovars bubbling away in the corner, Russian radio and TV broadcasting, and concerts by Berlin orchestras in which Russian musicians predominate. The Russians were at home in Berlin back at the beginning of the 20th century, and the turmoil of revolution brought almost the entire intellectual elite from St. Petersburg and Moscow to the River Spree. Since then Russian culture has been part of Berlin and has had an inspiring influence.

However, the most impressive element is the Jewish reincarnation of the Scheune district (the eastern part of the Spandau suburb) over the past few years. It was in 1866 that the first synagogue was opened here, and the magnificent dome, defiantly echoing the two other domes on the Palace and the Cathedral, became a guiding star for many Jewish migrants from Ukraine, Galicia and Russia driven out by pogroms and poverty. At one time the languages used in the Scheune district were Yiddish and Russian.

Virtually wiped out by the Holocaust, this culture is now gradually returning to its traditional district. There is a Jewish grammar school again, there are kosher restaurants, and a young, colourful, lively scene, comprising the descendants of those subjected to genocide. The Jewish revival of the Scheune district is almost like a fairytale, as it was so unexpected for so long – just like the glittering golden dome of the New Synagogue on Oranienburger Strasse, which was built between 1859 and 1866 in the Moresque Style.

Although Berlin has a newly emerging main centre, it is also shaped by its numerous local centres in the various districts. Their presence is explained by historical reasons and they make the development of the capital complex – yet they also lend the city a folkloric air by acting as hothouses of life and living.

S-Bahnhof Friedrichstraße.
Die mehr als 70-jährige Geschichte der Berliner S-Bahn-
höfe ist zugleich Spiegelbild
der Entwicklung Berlins.

Friedrichstrasse Station.
Berlin's suburban railway
stations have a 70-year
history which also reflects the
development of Berlin.

Prenzlauer Berg. Reges Treiben
herrscht in den Cafés am
Prenzlauer Berg, einem der
dichtbesiedelten Gebiete
Berlins. Kneipen und Kultur
lassen sich hier besonders inten-
siv erleben.

Prenzlauer Berg. It's all go in
the cafés on Prenzlauer Berg,
one of the most densely populated districts of Berlin, where
pubs and the arts scene combine to guarantee an exciting
experience.

42

Schöneberg. Markttag am Winterfeldtplatz.

Schöneberg. Market day on Winterfeldplatz.

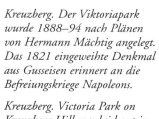

Kreuzberg. Der Viktoriapark wurde 1888–94 nach Plänen von Hermann Mächtig angelegt. Das 1821 eingeweihte Denkmal aus Gusseisen erinnert an die Befreiungskriege Napoleons.

Kreuzberg. Victoria Park on Kreuzberg Hill was laid out in 1888–94 to plans by Hermann Mächtig. Dedicated in 1821, the cast-iron monument commemorates Napoleon's Wars of Liberation.

Flohmarkt im Kietz.

Flea market in the Kietz.

Prenzlauer Berg. Eines der Zentren der Szene im Kiez ist der Kollwitzplatz.

Prenzlauer Berg. One of the hubs of the Kiez scene is Kollwitzplatz.

Kreuzberg. In Nachbarschaft des Berlin Museums steht das von Daniel Libeskind entworfene und 1999 eröffnete Neue Jüdische Museum.

Kreuzberg. The New Jewish Museum designed by Daniel Libeskind and opened in 1999 is located near the Berlin Museum.

45

City Ost gegen City West

Der Kampf um die neue Mitte ist unterhaltsam, aber entschieden

Als Berlin noch in zwei politische Systeme zerfiel, gehörte der Bezirk Mitte zum Ostteil der Stadt. Dort gab es, weil Mitte immer die Berliner Mitte gewesen ist, die meisten Berliner Sehenswürdigkeiten: das Brandenburger Tor, die Linden-Allee, die Oper, die Dome, die Synagoge, das Pergamon-Museum, den Invalidenfriedhof mit den Grabstätten berühmter Hauptstädter und vieles mehr. Zur DDR-Zeit kamen noch als Prestigebauten der Fernsehturm und der Palast der Republik hinzu. Die West-Berliner waren neidisch und klotzten ihre City West hoch. Savignyplatz, Kantstraße und vor allem Kurfürstendamm wurden regelrecht zu Stätten urbaner Präsentation aufgerüstet. Das beeindruckte Schulklassen aus Baden-Württemberg und rheinländische Touristen bei der obligatorischen Berlin-Visite und hielt die meisten davon ab, die lästige Grenzgänger-Prozedur auf sich zu nehmen. Sie hielten die City West für das Zentrum ganz Berlins, weil sie die City Ost nicht kannten.

Die City Ost war auch lange Zeit, und ist es teilweise heute noch, nicht gerade einladend mit ihren Waschbetonplatten von Gedenkstätten und Freizeiteinrichtungen, den Klötzen, die Kaufhallen genannt wurden, weil man den amerikanischen Begriff Supermarkt nicht mochte, und den Verkehrsschneisen, die zum Zweck von „Fließ- und Stehdemonstrationen" brachial mitten durch die alte Mitte Berlins geschlagen wurden. Aber wer es in die Seitenstraßen schaffte, in die Acker-, Mulack- oder Krausnickstraße und andere Straßen mit hoher Schlaglochdichte, war angerührt.

Reine Nostalgie kam zwar nicht auf beim Anblick zerlöcherter, rußiger Hausfassaden und offenstehender verrosteter Gittertore. Aber da waren auch Ladeninschriften aus der Vorkriegszeit, gab es in den HO- und Konsumläden noch die alten verschrammten Verkaufstheken, auf denen einst das Bonbonglas stand, war noch die alte rasselnde Kasse in Betrieb. Es hatte was, dieses Areal mit seinen vernagelten Kellereingängen, dem Bratfettgeruch aus Parterrefenstern, dem Unkraut zwischen den Quadersteinen, dem

East vs. West

The entertaining battle over the new centre is over

When Berlin was still divided into two political systems, the district of Central Berlin belonged to the eastern part. And being the centre, it was home to most of Berlin's sights: the Brandenburg Gate, the avenue Unter den Linden, the Opera House, the cathedrals, the synagogue, the Pergamon Museum, the Invalidenfriedhof cemetery containing the graves of famous Berliners, and many more besides. During the East German period, they were joined by prestige buildings like the TV Tower and the Palace of the Republic. Piqued, the West Berliners hit back by sprucing up their part of the city. Savignyplatz, Kantstrasse and above all Kurfürstendamm were elevated into places of urban spectacle. This was sufficiently impressive for school parties and tourists from West Germany during their obligatory sightseeing tours of Berlin that they didn't feel the need to go through the irksome process of crossing the border. Unaware of the city centre in the east, they thought this was the centre of Berlin.

It must be admitted that for a long time the centre of East Berlin was not especially inviting, and even nowadays there is still a lot of work to be done. It was full of memorials and concrete leisure facilities, retail monstrosities where usage of the American term 'supermarket' was shunned, and broad avenues hewn through the old centre to accommodate mass rallies. Yet those who managed to find their way into the old backstreets dotted with potholes like Ackerstrasse, Mulackstrasse or Krausnickstrasse and all the rest were moved.

It's true that the sight of sooty facades full of holes and open rusty iron gates didn't give rise to pure nostalgia. Yet memories were stirred by prewar shop inscriptions, by the old scratched counters where the jars of sweets used to stand and where the old rattling till was still used in the nationalised stores. The area had a certain something with its boarded-up cellar doors, the smell of cooking fat emanating from the ground-floor windows, the weeds squeezing out between the blocks of stone, the cool cellar smell with a hint of potatoes wafting out of the entrance gates,

Der in den Jahren 1966–1969 erbaute Fernsehturm zählt mit einer Höhe von 365 Metern zu den höchsten Bauwerken Europas.

The Fernsehturm, built between 1966 and 1969, is one of the tallest structures in Europe, standing 365 meters tall.

Die Statistiker haben den Überblick verloren. Die Senatsverwaltung für Kulturelle Angelegenheiten lässt deshalb Mitarbeiter gelegentlich alle örtlichen Programmzeitschriften, Flyer, Plakatwände und dergleichen begutachten, um eine Auflistung der kulturellen Aktivitäten zustandezubringen. Danach stehen in zwei Wochen durchschnittlich 400 Stücke an Berliner Bühnen zur Auswahl, 220 Kino-Filme, 200 laufende Galerie-Veranstaltungen sowie 120 Pop-Konzerte. Klassische Musik, Oper und Ballett schlagen mit 330 Aufführungen zu Buche. Die allsommerliche Love-Parade bringt geschätzte zwei Millionen Menschen auf die Beine

Attractions

Berlin's cultural life in figures
The statisticians have lost track. The Senate Cultural Affairs Administration therefore analyses all the local listings, arts magazines, leaflets and posters etc. in order to produce a list of current cultural activities. According to the results, every fortnight about 400 plays are performed in Berlin, 220 films are shown, there are 200 gallery events and 120 pop concerts, and 330 performances of classical music, opera and ballet. The Love Parade techno festival is attended by an estimated 2 million people every summer.

kühlen kartoffeligen Kellerhauch aus Toreinfahrten und den vermüllten Hinterhöfen mit den vielen Katzen und Hunden.

Diese Welt des Kleinbürgertums gibt es immer noch. Wer durch Berlin-Mitte läuft, dem gerät der Spaziergang zur Zeitreise. Selbst dort, wo der Bezirk zum Mahlstrom touristischer Invasion geworden ist, weil hier seit der Wende unaufhörlich neu-, auf- und umgebaut worden ist, erblickt man noch die Textur der Geschichte an Straßenverläufen und Häuserfassaden, das originale Berlin.

City Ost gegen City West. In den ersten Jahren nach der Wiedervereinigung hätte kaum jemand geglaubt, dass es so schnell zum unterhaltsamen Kampf der beiden Zentren kommen könnte. Der Westen besaß eine abgeschlossene Infrastruktur und lebte von der enorm starken Kaufkraft seiner Bewohner und Besucher. Der Osten konnte schon allein optisch nicht mithalten mit KaDeWe und Tauentzien, Ku'damm und dem Areal rings um den Bahnhof Zoo und den Breitscheidplatz. Dann aber kam der „Masterplan" für die City-Ost, ein Kniefall der Stadtplaner vor der gründerzeitlichen Metropole, die Erarbeitung eines „stadtbaukünstlerischen Regelwerks" für die historische Berliner Mitte mit den grundsätzlichen Aussagen: „Was wiederhergestellt werden muss, ist nicht weniger als die städtische Ordnung: dass die Schwerpunkte wieder an den richtigen Stellen liegen, Herz und zentrale Plätze der Stadt erkennbar sind... dass die neuen Formen wiedererkennbar sind als Übersetzung der nicht wiederherstellbaren historischen Formen."

Seitdem das „Planwerk Innenstadt" umgesetzt wird, ist der Osten im Kommen, während der Westen sich anstrengen muss, um mithalten zu können. Am deutlichsten wird das bei den Prachtboulevards Kurfürstendamm und Friedrichstraße, die um die Gunst der Kundschaft konkurrieren. Zwar ist in einer Millionenstadt Platz für zwei Renommierstraßen und belebt der Wettbewerb das Geschäft, aber hinter den Kulissen wird mit harten Bandagen gekämpft. Auch Traditionalisten sind mit von der Partie. Sie vertreten den Standpunkt: Wer den Ku'damm liebt, muss die Friedrichstraße ablehnen, und umgekehrt.

Der Kurfürstendamm geht in wesentlichen Teilen auf Reichskanzler Otto von Bismarck zurück, der, wie alle Regierenden, beseelt war, der Menschheit etwas Imposantes zu hinterlassen. Zwar gab es die Hauptstraße des Westens schon im 16. Jahrhundert, aber erst unter dem „Eisernen Kanzler", also ab 1875, in ihren heutigen Ausmaßen. In den 1880er Jahren entstanden

and littered backyards populated by cats and dogs.

This world of the petty bourgeoisie still exists. A walk through the centre of Berlin turns into a journey through time. Even where Berlin has become a maelstrom of tourist invasions drawn by the relentless refurbishment and construction since unification, the texture of history, the original Berlin, can still be perceived in the facades and the layout of the streets.

East vs. West. In the first few years after reunification, hardly anybody dreamed that an entertaining duel to was about to break out between the rival centres. West Berlin's infrastructure was complete and lived off the strong spending power of its population and visitors. Not even the appearance of the East could keep up with stores like KaDeWe, Tauentzien Palace, Kurfürstendamm and the area around the Zoo railway station, and Breitscheidplatz. But then came the "master plan" for the eastern centre, in which the city planners bowed down before the capital as it had been in the late 19th century. They drew up a "code of the art of town planning" for the historical centre of Berlin, the quintessence of which was: "What must be reinstated is nothing less than the urban order: the focal points must be in the right places again, the city's heart and its central squares must be recognisable.... The new forms must be a translation of the historical forms which cannot be restored."

Ever since the implementation of this plan for the city centre began, the East has been on the ascendant, while the West has been struggling to keep up. This is particularly apparent in the two magnificent boulevards Kurfürstendamm and Friedrichstrasse, which are now competing for customers. Although there is certainly room for two eminent boulevards in a city with a population of some three and a half million, and although competition stimulates business, behind the scenes the gloves are off. Traditionalists are joining in, taking the view that it is impossible to love both the "Ku'damm" and Friedrichstrasse.

We owe the main part of Kurfürstendamm to Bismarck, the Imperial Chancellor, who like all rulers was possessed by the idea of leaving mankind something impressive. Although it dates back to the 16th century, it was only under the "Iron Chancellor", i.e. from 1875 onwards, that it acquired its current dimensions, becoming the main street in the western part of Berlin. In the 1880s, the most magnificent houses in Germany were built here (complete with front gardens), and the road was given pavements four yards wide, a central promenade and bridle-path. The buildings featured broad marble stairways,

hier die prachtvollsten Häuser Deutschlands, mit Vorgärten, vier Meter breiten Gehwegen, Mittelpromenade und Reitweg. Es gab breite Marmortreppen, Säulen und Glasfenster wie in Kathedralen zu bestaunen. Die schillerndsten Kaffeehäuser öffneten, das berühmteste von allen war das Romanische Café. 1921 gab das Theater am Kurfürstendamm die erste Premiere, 1922 wurde im Alhambra der erste Kinofilm der Welt aufgeführt. Der Zweite Weltkrieg zerstörte von 230 Prachtgebäuden ganze 180. Zwar wurden die Lücken gefüllt, doch der Glanz nicht wieder hergestellt. Eindrucksvoll ist das bunte Gemisch des Straßenzuges. Er ist zur Bummel-, Shopping- und „Fressmeile" mit breitgefächertem Kultur- und Vergnügungsangebot geworden.

In dieser Hinsicht will die Friedrichstraße nicht zurückstecken, hier wird mit mondänen Kaufhäusern, dem Dussmann-Kulturkaufhaus oder dem Friedrichstadtpalast, dem größten Revuetheater Europas, ebenfalls ein Strauß von

columns and glass windows, putting them on a par with cathedrals. Splendid coffee houses opened, the most famous of them being the Romanesque Café. In 1921, the theatre on Kurfürstendamm presented its first première, and in 1922 the first cinema film in the world was shown in the Alhambra. Yet during World War II, 180 of the 230 magnificent buildings were destroyed. Although the gaps have since been filled, the old glamour has not been restored. Nevertheless, the kaleidoscopic street life is still impressive. Kurfürstendamm has become a boulevard for strolling, shopping and eating out offering a host of cultural and entertainment facilities.

In this respect, Friedrichstrasse intends to make sure it does not lag behind. Its fashionable department stores, the Dussmann art emporium and Friedrichstadtpalast, the biggest European revue theatre, all mean that visitors are never short of things to do. The street is two miles long

Charlottenburg. Die Plastik „Berlin" in der Tauentzienstraße gewährt den Blick auf die als Mahnmal belassene Ruine der Kaiser-Wilhelm-Gedächtniskirche am Breitscheidplatz.

Charlottenburg. The sculpture entitled "Berlin" on Tauentzienstrasse provides a view over the ruins of the Kaiser Wilhelm Church of Remembrance on Breitscheidplatz, which has been left untouched as a memorial.

49

*Friedrichshain. Ursprünglich
als Industriekomplex errichtet,
erfuhr der Treptower 1979
und 1994 bauliche Veränder-
ungen und ist zur Zeit das
höchste Bürogebäude der Stadt.*

*Friedrichshain. Originally
constructed as industrial
complex, the Treptower was
given a thorough face-lift in
1979 and 1994 and is
currently the world's tallest
office building.*

Offerten überreicht. 3,3 Kilometer lang ist die Straße, benannt nach dem Preußenkönig Fried-rich I., der sie Anfang des 18. Jahrhunderts als schlichte Wohnstraße errichten ließ. Schnell avancierte sie zur Geschäftsstraße und verruch-ten Vergnügungsmeile, berühmte Leute wohn-ten hier, angefangen von dem herausragenden Arzt Christoph Wilhelm Hufeland, den Schrift-stellern Heinrich Kleist und Victor von Scheffel, dem Philosophen Johann Gottlieb Fichte oder dem Schauspieler und Regisseur Max Reinhardt. Nach einem schweren Bombenangriff im Feb-ruar 1945 war die Straße ein Trümmerhaufen. In den achtziger Jahren wollte sie der SED-Staat als Gegenstück zum Kurfürstendamm aufpäppeln. Nun ist sie in wesentlichen Teilen erneuert und sehr attraktiv.

Die Konkurrenz wird weiter beschworen wer-den, aber der Kampf ist entschieden. Investoren, Touristen und die Einheimischen selbst haben ihre Sympathien klar verteilt. Die alte Mitte wird die neue Mitte sein, auch wenn dort noch sehr viel zu tun ist. Alle zieht es in Renzo Pianos erd-farbene High-Tech-Stadt, zur neuen Friedrich-straße und an den schönsten Platz Berlins, den Gendarmenmarkt. Er ist auch nach seiner Neu-gestaltung noch geschichtsträchtig, der Weltrei-sende Georg Forster nannte ihn einst den „schönsten Platz der Welt". Die identisch monu-mentalen Kuppeltürme des Deutschen und des Französischen Doms und Schinkels Schauspiel-haus mit seiner markanten Schaufront sorgen für eben die Theatralik, die den Gendarmenmarkt zu einem einmaligen Platz macht. Das histori-sche Ensemble ist gesäumt von einer betont modernen Platzrandgestaltung, in der auch das erste Select-Hotel der Dorint-Gruppe unterge-bracht ist. Ein designverliebtes Haus, das mit überraschenden Effekten in seinen Bann zieht und den Aufenthalt darin zum sinnlichen Erleb-nis werden lässt.

Der „neue" Hackesche Markt hat sich in Re-kordtempo zum Dreh- und Angelpunkt von Berlinern und Besuchern entwickelt, zum Zen-tralgestirn des neuen Berlin und – mit seinem Straßenumfeld und dem Monbijou-Park – zum Bermudadreieck des Nachtlebens. Die Hacke-schen Höfe – ein 80-Millionen-Sanierungspro-jekt – sind ein Geflecht von acht miteinander verbundenen Hinterhöfen, die in der Wende-zeit zum 20. Jahrhundert Platz boten für Klein-gewerbe, Handwerk, Gastronomie und Klein-kunst. Seit 1995 sind Restaurants, Kneipen, Bühnen und Galerien wieder da und zeigen sich im Märchenglanz von blau und rot glasier-tem Klinker. Der stark gegliederte Baukörper schwingt sich um zwei Straßenecken, die mit

and was named after Frederick I of Prussia, who had it built at the beginning of the 18th century as a modest residential street. It rapidly developed into a business street and a seedy pleasure district. Famous people lived here, such as the outstanding doctor Christoph Wil-helm Hufeland, the writers Heinrich Kleist and Victor von Scheffel, the philosopher Johann Gottlieb Fichte, and the actor and director Max Reinhardt. During a severe air raid in February

1945, the street was reduced to a heap of rubble. In the 1980s, the East German state decided to revitalise it as a counterpart to Kurfürstendamm. Much of it has since been redeveloped and is now very attractive.

Although the competition may still continue to be stoked, the battle is already over. Investors, tourists and the locals themselves have already voted with their feet. The old centre will be the new centre, even if there is still plenty to be done. Everyone's flocking to Renzo Piano's earth-coloured high-tech city, to the new Friedrich-strasse and to Gendarmenmarkt – Berlin's most beautiful square. Despite being restyled, it still remains steeped in history. World traveller Georg Forster once described it as the "most beautiful square in the world". The identical monumental dome-shaped roofs of the German and French cathedrals and Schinkel's Theatre with its prominent facade conjure up the theatri-cal effect which make Gendarmenmarkt into a unique square. The historical ensemble is framed by buildings with a markedly modern style. They include the first Select Hotel of the Dorint Group, whose fanciful design employs some surprising effects to catch the eye and turns every stay into a sheer experience for the senses.

In record time, the "new" Hackescher Markt has become a top attraction for Berliners and visit-ors, the focus of the new Berlin and – with its surrounding streets and the Monbijou Park – the Bermuda triangle of night-life. Hackesche Höfe, a DM 80 million redevelopment project, is a

Metall gedeckten Mansard- und Tonnendächer, die Gesimse, Kapitelle und das angedeutete Pilaster für eine freischwebend-klassizistische Fassadengliederung bringen jeden Betrachter zum Entzücken. Naturstein, Glas und Putz wechseln ab, kräftig rot und grün getönt, aber auch matt zwischen Sand und Grau changierend. Die gewachsene Kleinteiligkeit der ursprünglichen Höfe wird auch dort, wo Neubauteile eingefügt wurden, durch eine bewegte Dachgaubenlandschaft, unterschiedliche Fensterformen und andere liebevolle Details mit entschiedenem Willen unterstrichen. Der vom Stadtkommandanten Graf von Hacke um die Mitte des 18. Jahrhunderts angelegte Marktplatz ist wieder zu einem urbanen Ort geworden.

Ganz so einfach wird es der Alexanderplatz, die große zurückgelassene Stadtbrache des Realsozialismus, nicht haben. Noch wirkt er „wie ein Vorposten der Mongolei, seine Leere und Weite spiegeln die östliche Mangelökonomie, deren einziges Luxusprodukt die maßlose Raumverschwendung war" (FAZ). Doch der Umbau des „Alex" ist beschlossene Sache. Für Architekten eine völlig neue Herausforderung: Während Plätze bisher dadurch entstanden, dass Grundstücke abgeräumt oder freigehalten wurden, ist hier massive Bebauung und Umgrenzung der Freiflächen das einzige probate Mittel, städtische Dichte zu erreichen. Zwar kann das neue Konzept, das einen Ausbau des Platzes zu einem kleinen Wolkenkratzer-Downtown vorsieht, das alte Spinnennetz der Straßen nicht wieder herstellen. Aber das grobschlächtige Achsenkreuz als Aufmarschfläche für Paraden wird beseitigt, menschliche Maßstäbe werden für den Umbau angelegt. Die Bauzeit allerdings wird mit mindestens 20 Jahren angegeben.

Mehrere Blöcke, bis zu 30 Meter hoch, sollen zu einer abgetreppten Turmgruppe vereint werden. Steinkaskaden als Reverenz an den Klassizismus sollen in den Berliner Himmel emporschießen. Entstehen soll ein funktionstüchtiges Metropolenviertel, das Leben und Arbeiten, Wohnen und Shoppen auf harmonische Weise vereint. Die vertikale Hochverdichtung wird Berlin-Mitte ein großstädtisches Viertel bescheren, wie es das bisher noch nie hatte. Die Annäherung an das New Yorker Vorbild, obgleich nur im kleinen, begrenzten Rahmen, wird etwas gänzlich Neues für Berlin darstellen und den Metropolencharakter verstärken.

Was mit dem Herzen der Berliner Mitte geschieht, dem Schlossplatz mit dem Palast der Republik, ist noch nicht entschieden. Aber die bisherige Baurichtung stimmt optimistisch, die City Ost ist im Aufschwung.

dense network of eight interconnected backyards housing small businesses, craft outlets, restaurants and cabarets. Since 1995 restaurants, pubs, venues and art galleries have returned, dressed in a fairytale sheen of blue and red glazed bricks. Visitors are amazed by the heavily structured building arching around two corners, the metal-covered mansard and tunnel roofs, the cornices, capitals and the suggested pilaster for a classicist facade structure. Natural stone, glass and plaster alternate with each other, sometimes with a strong red or green tint, and sometimes soft and shimmering between sand and grey. The organic partitioning of the original courtyards is even emphasised in the new sections by the variation of dormer windows, various window forms and other loving details. The market square laid out in the mid-18th century by Count von Hacke, the city commandant, has turned back into an urban centre.

Things won't be as easy for Alexanderplatz, the huge expanse of wasteland left behind by the collapse of Actually Existing Socialism. It still looks "... like an outpost of Mongolia, its emptiness and expanse reflecting the economy of shortages prevailing in the East, whose only luxury product was the excessive waste of space." (Frankfurter Allgemeine Zeitung) However, the reconstruction of "Alex" has already been decided. Architects are faced by a totally new challenge. Whereas in the past squares were created by demolishing properties and keeping land free of development, in this case massive development and enclosing the open space is the only effective method to achieve the required urban density. Even if the new plan ordaining the conversion of the square into a small district of skyscrapers cannot re-establish the old spider's web of streets, the broad axes providing space for parades will be eliminated.

Several blocks up to 33 yards tall are to be united to form a crow-stepped tower group. Stone cascades paying tribute to classicism will shoot up into the Berlin sky. The plan is to create a functional city district harmoniously blending living, working and shopping. This vertical increase in density will provide central Berlin with the city district it has never had before. This adoption of key aspects from New York's example will be something entirely new for Berlin and will boost its metropolitan character.

Exactly what will be done with the heart of central Berlin, Schlossplatz (containing the Palace of the Republic), has still to be decided. Yet the current progress of construction activities is highly promising. The eastern centre is undergoing major revival.

Erlebnis

Gendarmenmarkt
Das festliche Ensemble ist ein Prachtstück klassizistischer Baukunst.
An den schönsten Platz Berlins grenzen Schinkels Schauspielhaus (Konzerthaus Berlin), der Deutsche und Französische Dom, die Akademie der Wissenschaften Berlin-Brandenburg und die Hanns-Eisler-Hochschule für Musik. Das Schiller-Denkmal in der Platzmitte stammt von Reinhold Begas (1871), die Zitate im Pflaster vor dem Schauspielhaus stammen von Beethoven, Schiller, Lortzing, Glasbrenner und Hegel

Alexanderplatz
Weltzeituhr, Brunnen der Völkerfreundschaft, Berolinahaus, Alexanderhaus, S- und U-Bahn-Station, Kaufhäuser

Attractions

Gendarmenmarkt
This festive ensemble is a gem of classical architecture. Berlin's most beautiful square is bordered by Schinkel's Schauspielhaus Theatre (Berlin Concert Hall), the German and French cathedrals, the Berlin–Brandenburg Academy of Sciences, and Hans Eisler College of Music. The monument to Schiller in the middle of the square is the work of Reinhold Begas (1871), while the quotations in the pavement in front of the Schauspielhaus stem from Beethoven, Schiller, Lortzing, Glasbrenner and Hegel.

Alexanderplatz
World Clock, International Friendship Fountain, Berolina House, Alexander House, railway station (overground/underground), department stores.

Das Bodemuseum als Teil der Museumsinsel entstand in den Jahren 1897–1904.
Derzeit wird es umgebaut und nicht vor 2004 wiedereröffnet.

The Bode Museum was built as part of Museum Island in 1897–1904.
Currently being refurbished, it is not due to be reopened before 2004.

Der Alexanderplatz, benannt nach dem russischen Zaren Alexander I., ist heute
Fußgängerzone. Die Weltzeituhr von Erich John (1969) gehört neben dem Forum-Hotel
zu den Sehenswürdigkeiten des Platzes.

Alexanderplatz, named after Russian Tsar Alexander I, is now a pedestrian area.
Sights on the square include the 1969 World Clock designed by Erich John, and
the Forum Hotel.

Open-Air-Konzert mit dem
Berliner Symphonie-Orchester
vor dem Schauspielhaus auf
dem Gendarmenmarkt.

Open-air concert by the Berlin
Symphony Orchestra in front
of the Schauspielhaus theatre
on Gendarmenmarkt.

Der Friedrichstadtpalast ist
das größte Revuetheater
Europas.

Friedrichstadtpalast is the
largest revue theatre in Europe.

53

Das Märkische Museum im Stil der märkischen Backstein-gotik wurde 1874 gegründet.

The Mark Museum in the brick Gothic style from Mark Brandenburg was established in 1874.

Der Volkspark Friedrichshain zählt zu den größten Parkanlagen der Innenstadt.

Volkspark Friedrichshain is one of the largest parks in the city centre.

Zwischen 1980–87 entstand unter Einbeziehung noch erhaltener und rekonstruierter Gebäude des 18.–20. Jahr-hunderts zwischen Spreeufer, Mühlendamm, Spandauer Straße und Rathausstraße das Nikolaiviertel.

The Nikolaiviertel district was built in 1980–87 and included both preserved and reconstructed buildings from the 18–20th centuries between Spreeufer, Mühlendamm, Spandauer Strasse and Rathausstrasse.

Die Hackeschen Höfe, Deutschlands größter Wohn- und Gewerbehof, sind ein Labyrinth aus acht Höfen und heute Szenetreff mit Kneipen, Läden und Kino.

Hackesche Höfe, Germany's largest combined residential and commercial complex, is a labyrinth comprising eight courtyards which has become a popular meeting place featuring pubs, shops and cinemas.

Hackesche Höfe. Antiquitäten finden hier ihre Liebhaber.

Hackesche Höfe. Antiques are quickly snapped up by collectors.

Das DORINT Am Gendarmenmarkt in Berlin Mitte.

Hotel DORINT Am Gendarmenmarkt in Berlin Mitte.

57

Die St.-Hedwigs-Kathedrale am Bebelplatz,
1747–73 als barocker Zentralbau nach Vorbild
des römischen Pantheons erbaut, ist seit 1929
die Kirche des katholischen Bistums Berlins.

St. Hedwig's Cathedral on Bebelplatz, built in
1747–73 as a central baroque building and
modelled on the Roman Pantheon, has since 1929
been the church of the Catholic Diocese of Berlin.

Die unter der 74 Meter hohen Kuppel gelegene
Predigtkirche im Berliner Dom bietet 2100
Personen Platz.

Predigtkirche situated beneath the 80-yard dome
of Berlin Cathedral seats 2,100.

Der Berliner Dom an der Ostseite des Lustgartens
wurde in den Jahren 1894–1904 nach Ent-
würfen von Julius Raschdorf als „Hauptkirche des
preußischen Protestantismus" errichtet.

Berlin Cathedral to the east of the pleasance
was erected in 1894–1904 after being designed
by Julius Raschdorf as the "main church of
Prussian Protestantism".

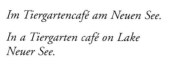

Am Kurfürstendamm herrscht zu jeder Tages- und Jahreszeit reges Treiben.

Kurfürstendamm's always full of bustling activity the whole year round.

Im Tiergartencafé am Neuen See.

In a Tiergarten café on Lake Neuer See.

Die Kongresshalle im Tiergarten – heute „Haus der Kulturen der Welt".

The congress hall in Tiergarten, now known as the "House of World Cultures".

Love Parade. Hunderttausende Raver tummeln sich bei der jährlich im Sommer stattfindenden größten Techno-Party der Welt.

The Love Parade. The largest techno party in the world is attended by hundreds of thousands of ravers every summer.

61

Der Flughafen „Otto Lilienthal" in Tegel, 1948 Versorgungsflughafen während der Berlin-Blockade, wurde in den Jahren 1969–71 zu einem der modernsten europäischen Passagierflughäfen umgebaut.

Otto Lilienthal Airport in Tegel rose to fame in 1948 during the Berlin Blockade. In 1969–71 it was converted into one of the most modern passenger airports in Europe.

Verkehrsknotenpunkt am Internationalen Congress Centrum (ICC).

Junction at the ICC (International Congress Centre).

Die 138 Meter hohe und etwa
400 Tonnen schwere Stahl-
konstruktion des Funkturms
entstand in den Jahren
1924–26. Ursprünglich als
reiner Antennenmast angelegt,
erhielt er nachträglich ein
Restaurant und eine Aussichts-
plattform.

Over 150 yards tall and
weighing around 400 tons,
the steel construction of the
radio tower was built in
1924–26. Originally designed
as a simple antenna, a restaurant and a viewing platform
were subsequently added.

Charlottenburg. Das Olympia-
Stadion bietet beinahe 90.000
Besuchern Platz.

Charlottenburg. The Olympic
Stadium seats nearly 90,000.

Das Olympia-Stadion wurde
1934–36 gebaut und zur
Fußball-Weltmeisterschaft 1974
renoviert und modernisiert.

The Olympic Stadium was
built in 1934–36 and was
refurbished in time for the
1974 World Cup.

Seiten 64/65
Weihnachtlicher Trubel rund
um den Breitscheidplatz und
die Gedächtniskirche.

Christmas rush around
Breitscheidplatz and the
Remembrance Church.

63

Es fährt kein Sonderzug mehr nach Pankow

Die Bezirke an der Peripherie der Berliner Mitte präsentieren sich

Die Panke fließt in Richtung Westen. Nach dem Flüsschen ist der Berliner Bezirk benannt, der in Zeiten des Kalten Krieges mit dem DDR-Regime gleichgesetzt wurde. Pankow war ein Synonym für den Funktionärsstaat, und die ranghohen Bedenkenträger wohnten auch großteils hier, in der Gegend um den Majakowski-Ring, bis sie in die hermetisch abgeriegelte Waldsiedlung bei Wandlitz umzogen. Dieses Image, Hochburg der Bonzen zu sein, haben die Pankower gründlich beseitigt. Sie knüpfen lieber wieder an die Zeit davor an, als der Berliner Nordosten eine feine Adresse war. Und für Udo Lindenberg, der mit Honecker „einen draufmachen" wollte, gibt es keinen Sonderzug mehr.

Um die Wende zum 20. Jahrhundert war Pankow mit vielen Parks und Gartenlokalen ein beliebtes Ausflugsziel. Man verglich es mit Schwabing oder dem Montmartre. Vor allem das Berliner „Philistertum", Künstler, aber auch Lebenskünstler, fühlten sich angezogen. In diese Zeit fällt auch der Bau der vielen Villen, die Berliner Unternehmer ihren Familien errichten ließen. Frau und Kinder sollten an der frischen Luft sein, umgeben von Grün. Bis dahin war der Ort nur ein Kaff, die alte Dorfkirche, ein Feldsteinbau, stammte aus dem 14. Jahrhundert. 1859 war nach Plänen von Friedrich August Stüler ein dreischiffiger Ziegelbau hinzugekommen. Das Gotteshaus markiert das eine Ende des Marktes, am anderen Ende das prachtvolle, ziegelrote Rathaus, Jugendstil mit Neobarock-Anklängen. In der nahegelegenen Görschstraße stehen einige der schönsten Berliner Schulhäuser der Gründerzeit. Die Wollankstraße, benannt nach einer vermögenden Pankower Familie, war die Ausfallstrecke in den Westen, nach Gesundbrunnen und Reinickendorf.

In Pankow ist durch Paul Nipkow das Fernsehen erfunden worden, das erste Filmvorführgerät und die Thermosflasche. Die kreativen Geister von einst liegen mit anderen Lokal- und Weltberühmtheiten auf Pankower Friedhöfen. Pankows schönste Hervorbringung sind aber Bürger- und Schlosspark. Dort prunkt das Schloss Niederschönhausen, dessen erste

The special train to Pankow's been cancelled

The self-assured districts surrounding central Berlin

The small River Panke flows westwards. It gave its name to the district of Pankow, which during the Cold War was equated with the East German regime. Pankow was a synonym for the functionaries' state, and those in charge mainly lived here in the area around Majakowski-Ring before moving to a more isolated locality near Wandlitz. The inhabitants of Pankow have since completely done away with this image of being the stronghold of party bigwigs. They prefer to associate themselves with the previous era, when the north-eastern part of Berlin used to be an upmarket location. Udo Lindenberg used to sing about "painting the town red" with Erich Honecker and the special train to Pankow – but in the new timetable it's been cancelled.

Around the turn of the 20th century, Pankow with its many parks and pub gardens used to be a popular destination for day trippers. It was often compared to Schwabing in Munich or the Parisian Montmartre. The place held a special attraction for the Berlin Philistines – artists, but also experts in the art of living. This was the time when many Berlin industrialists had villas built here for their families. They wanted their wives and children to be out in the fresh air, surrounded by greenery.

Previously the place had been just a dead-and-alive hole with a 14th-century village church made of boulders to which in 1859 a brick building with a nave and two aisles was added by Friedrich August Stüler. This place of worship marks one end of the marketplace; the other end is dominated by the magnificent, brick-red town hall built in *Jugendstil* (Germany's answer to art nouveau) with neo-Baroque echoes. The nearby Görschstrasse contains some of Berlin's most beautiful school buildings dating back to the late 19th century. Wollankstrasse, named after a wealthy Pankow family, was once the main road leading westwards out of the city towards Gesundbrunnen and Reinickendorf.

It was in Pankow that Paul Nipkow invented television, the first film projector, and the Thermos flask. The creative spirits of the past lie alongside other local and international celebrities

Zehlendorf. Der Große Wannsee bedeckt eine Fläche von 260 ha. Er gilt mit seinem 80 m breiten und 1300 m langen Sandstrand als größtes europäisches Binnenseebad.

Zehlendorf. Lake Wannsee covers an area of 640 acres. With a beach measuring 90 yards wide and 1,450 yards long, it is one of Europe's largest lakeside resorts.

Mauern schon um 1650 gestanden haben sollen. Bis 1960 war es Sitz des Präsidenten und später des Staatsrates der DDR, danach Gästesitz für Castro, Gorbatschow, Arafat und andere Staatsgäste. Der heutige Bau entstand nach Plänen von Göthe, einem Schüler Schlüters. Die Preußenkönige nutzten das Schloss als Sommerresidenz und schoben gern ihre Frauen dorthin ab. Es gibt lustige Geschichten darüber, was sich bei „Königs" alles abgespielt haben soll. Ein englischer Diplomat wusste in einem Brief zu vermelden, die preußischen Prinzessinnen seien keine Spielverderberinnen und von trefflicher Gesundheit. Bei den Pankowern waren sie beliebt, weil sie sich wohltätig zeigten und für Arbeiterfamilien hygienische Wohnverhältnisse schufen. So wurde eine Königinplantage angelegt und bedürftigen Paaren im Schloss die Hochzeit ausgerichtet.

Heute ist das Schloss mit dem getäfelten Arbeitszimmer von Wilhelm Pieck, Gorbatschows Schlafgemach und den Schäferszenen im Damenzimmer zu besichtigen. Der Park gehört seit der Wende wieder den Menschen und ist nicht mehr gegen sie abgeriegelt. Kinder waten durch das Laub uralter Bäume, Liebespaare dösen über ihrem Glück auf den Wiesen, während Eichhörnchen im Geäst darüber Kapriolen hinlegen. Pankow gehört zu den Stadtbezirken, die seit der Wende an Bevölkerung zugelegt haben. Nach dem schwachen Abgang der Parteifunktionäre ist es wieder eine Top-Adresse.

Berlin hat mehrere Top-Adressen außerhalb seines großflächigen Zentrums. Alle Stadtbezirke haben viel Grün, die meisten viel Wasser und bessere Luft. Manche der ehemaligen Vorstädte besitzen zudem den Charme der Wohnquartiere aus der Gründerzeit. Nachdem der Wohnungsbau der Nachkriegszeit im Osten wie Westen wuchernde Streusiedlungen und triste Hochhaus-Ghettos hervorgebracht hatte, wird nun ganz anders geplant und projektiert. Großinvestoren eifern bewährten Vorbildern aus dem 19. Jahrhundert nach. Da wird verdichtet, Rücksicht genommen auf die Natur, aber auch Neues gewagt. Das Modellprojekt ist Karow-Nord, eine Mustersiedlung kalifornischer Stadtarchitekten im flachen Acker- und Wiesenland des Berliner Nordens. Mietshäuser, Wohnzeilen und Stadtvillen mit drei bis vier Geschossen und der dazugehörigen kompletten Infrastruktur sind hier nach altem Berliner Baumuster entstanden. Die Kohorten von Bauträgern und Abschreibungsprofis, die andernorts ihre Wohnparks, Büro- und Einkaufscenter wie loses Stückgut auf den Feldern abluden, hatten hier keine Chance und werden keine haben.

in Pankow's cemeteries. Yet Pankow's most exquisite creation is the park housing the magnificent Niederschönhausen Palace, whose first walls are said to have been built in the mid-17th century. Until 1960 it was the seat of first the East German President and then the Council of State. Later it was used as a guesthouse for Fidel Castro, Mikhail Gorbachev, Yasser Arafat and other state guests.

The present building was erected to plans drawn up by Göthe, a student of Schlüter. The Prussian kings used the palace as their summer residence and as a place where their wives could be kept out of the way. Amusing tales abound concerning what went on among the royals. For example, an English diplomat wrote in a letter that the Prussian princesses were "game for anything" and "in prime condition". What's more, the royals were popular with the inhabitants of Pankow because they were charitable and tried to establish hygienic living conditions for working class families. A plantation was laid out for the Prussian queens, and the weddings of needy couples were organised in the palace.

Nowadays, the Palace is a museum where visitors can see the panelled office of Wilhelm Pieck (the first East German President), Gorbachev's bedroom, and the pastoral scenes in the ladies' room. Since unification, the park has been returned to the public and is no longer fenced off. Children wade through the leaves of ancient trees, courting couples doze happily on the grass, with squirrels above them cutting capers in the branches. Pankow is one of the districts of Berlin whose population has actually grown since reunification. Following the departure of the party bosses, it has now become a prime location again.

Berlin now has several prime locations outside its large centre. All the districts have large green spaces, and most of them also have stretches of water and cleaner air. Moreover, some of the former suburbs still possess the charm of the late-19th-century residential areas. After postwar housing development spewed forth scattered estates and dreary ghettos of high-rise buildings in both East and West Berlin, planning has now completely altered. Large investors are emulating proven models from the 19th century. In addition to increasing density and paying attention to nature, they are also risking some innovative approaches. The North Karow model project designed by Californian urban architects has been implemented on the flat farmland and meadows north of Berlin. Blocks of rented flats, terraced houses and town villas with three or four storeys along with the entire infrastructure have been built here using old Berlin building

Die aufgelockerten Blöcke mit klar konturierten Höfen, Straßen und Plätzen schaffen eine Dramaturgie von öffentlichen und privaten Räumen, wie sie für das Berlin der Gründerzeit typisch und vorbildlich war. Für 2,5 Milliarden Mark entstand ein gemischtes Wohngebiet mit ganz unterschiedlichen Wohneinheiten, mit Kindertagesstätten, Schulen, Jugendeinrichtungen und Sportmöglichkeiten. Auch den Bäcker gibt es im neuen Kiez, den Metzger und den Blumenladen. Die Weimarer Gartenstadt-Idee stand Pate bei diesem Modell.

Anders entwickelt sich Adlershof, von wo einst das DDR-Fernsehen mit dem Sandmännchen den Jüngsten virtuellen Traumsand in die Augen streute. Geträumt wird nicht mehr, denn Adlershof soll das deutsche Silicon Valley werden. Als Wissenschaftsstandort hat der Bezirk Tradition: 1909 fand hier die erste Internationale Luftfahrtschau der Welt statt, es gab Forschungs-, Militär- und Fernseheinrichtungen. Auf einem 420 Hektar großen Areal, umarmt von S-Bahn-Gleisen und dem Teltow-Kanal, entsteht eine multifunktionale Stadtlandschaft, die neben dem Wissenschaftspark Wisba eine neue Medien-City und umfangreichen Wohnungsneubau aufweisen wird. Schon spricht man von der „Wissenschaftsstadt" Adlershof. Sandmännchens Geburtsort ist doch noch ein Platz der Träume, den Kindern wird hier ihre Zukunft bereitet.

Auch die Wasserstadt am Spandauer See, zwischen Charlottenburg und dem Spandauer Forst, direkt an den Ufern der Havel, macht von sich reden. Lange führte das riesige Gelände ein Schattendasein als Industriebrache. Demnächst werden hier 34 000 Menschen in einem zum Wasser hin orientierten Wohngebiet leben. Auch Köpenick und Friedrichshagen, als südöstliche Berliner Stadtbezirke bisher wenig in Erscheinung getreten, Weißensee, Tempelhof oder Schöneberg zeigen nach historischen Brüchen, Neuanfängen und Widersprüchlichkeiten Profil. Die Berliner Bezirke, bis zur Wende nur lose miteinander verbunden, haben Häutungen hinter sich, die ihre wahre Gestalt zum Vorschein gebracht haben. Der Zerfall der DDR und die deutsche Wiedervereinigung haben keiner Stadt so viele Überraschungen beschert wie Berlin. Die Stadt mit ihrer bewegten und bewegenden Geschichte entsteht in atemberaubendem Tempo neu, lebt aber als Stadtlandschaft mit unterschiedlichen Bezirken von ihren Kontrasten. „Berlin ist schön, Berlin ist groß", schrieb schon Alfred Kerr. Das trifft nun, nach dem Ende der widernatürlichen Teilung, wieder zu. Berlin ist zu einer Stadt für jedermann geworden. Eine Stadt – auf dem Weg zur Metropole.

patterns. The cohorts of developers and depreciation pros who elsewhere dumped their residential parks, offices and shopping centres on the fields like sacks of potatoes had no chance. The loosely structured blocks with clearly outlined courtyards, streets and squares create a design of public and private spaces typical of Berlin in the late 19th century. A mixed residential area with very different types of housing, a kindergarten and nursery complex, schools, youth and sports facilities – not to mention a baker's, a butcher's and a flower shop – have been built for DM2.5 billion. The Weimar garden town concept served as a model for this project. Other districts, such as Adlershof, developed very differently. Adlershof used to be the headquarters of East German TV – where the Sandman used to sprinkle sand into the eyes of the very young. But it has now put its sleepy past behind it, for Adlershof is to become the German Silicon Valley. The district has a history of science, hosting back in 1909 the world's first international aviation show, and being home to research, military and television facilities. A multifunctional urban landscape is springing up on more than 180 acres framed by railway tracks and Teltow Canal, which will house the Wisba Science Park and a new Media City, as well as numerous new residential buildings. In fact Adlershof is already being referred to as "Science City". After all, it's only right that the birthplace of the Sandman should also be a location full of dreams – a place where our children's future is being prepared.

The water town at Lake Spandau, between Charlottenburg and Spandau Forest, right on the banks of the River Havel, is also making a name for itself. For decades, this huge area led a shadowy existence as an industrial wasteland – but very soon about 34,000 people will live here in a waterside residential area.

The south-eastern Berlin districts of Köpenick and Friedrichshagen, little noticed in the past, as well as Weissensee, Tempelhof and Schöneberg, are starting to emerge as well following a troubled past. Berlin's districts, only loosely connected before unification, have shed their skins and are now showing their true identity. The disintegration of East Germany and German reunification have brought forth more surprises in Berlin than in any other city. Possessed of an eventful and moving history, the city is ascending at breathtaking speed, while its urban landscape thrives on its vivid contrasts. It's a development which is perhaps best summed up by Alfred Kerr: "Berlin is beautiful, Berlin is great."

Die Glienicker Brücke verbindet Berlin mit Potsdam und durfte bis Anfang 1990 nur von den Alliierten passiert werden.

Glienicker Bridge, which links Berlin with Potsdam, could only be used by the Allies until the beginning of 1990.

Ein beliebtes Ausflugsziel der Berliner ist Tegel mit seinem Humboldt-Schlösschen, dem Tegelner Forst und dem Tegelner See.

Tegel with its Humboldt-Schlösschen (Humboldt Palace), the Tegel Forest and Tegel Lake is a favorite place for Berliners to go on outings.

Im Britzer Garten. Berlin ist reich an grünen Oasen.

Britz Garden. Just one of Berlin's many green oases.

Auch der Pferdesport hat Tradition in Berlin und zieht jährlich Tausende von Besuchern an.

Horse-Racing goes back a long way in Berlin and attracs thousands of visitors every year.

Tiergarten. Restaurantschiff auf dem Landwehrkanal.

Tiergarten. Restaurant ship on the Landwehrkanal.

Steglitz. 1897 wurde hier der Botanische Garten angelegt. Zu seinen Attraktionen gehören heute das Botanische Museum, der Kurfürstliche Garten und ein Duft -und Tastgarten.

Steglitz. The Botanical Gardens were laid out here in 1897. Their modern-day attractions include the Botanical Museum, the Royal Garden, and a fragrance and touch garden for the blind.

Steglitz. Im Botanischen Garten blüht die Victoria regia, deren riesige Schwimmblätter 80 kg Last tragen können.

Steglitz. The Victoria regia can be seen in the Botanical Gardens. These huge floating leaves look like flan bases and can weigh as much as 175 pounds.

Das zwischen 1695 und 1746 entstandene Charlottenburger Schloss ist ein Beispiel für die Baukunst der preußischen Könige.

Built between 1695 and 1746, Charlottenburg Palace is an example of the architecture of the Prussian kings.

Zehlendorf. Der von der Havel durchflossene Große Wannsee ist eines der beliebtesten Erholungszentren der Berliner.

Zehlendorf. Lake Grosse Wannsee through which the River Havel flows is one of the most popular recreation areas for Berliners.

*Zehlendorf. Schinkel baute das ehemalige Gutshaus in ein
klassizistisches Schloss im Stil eines römischen Landhauses um.
Das Schloss Klein-Glienicke ist umgeben von einem
100 ha großen Landschaftsgarten, der durch Peter Lenné
angelegt wurde.*

*Zehlendorf. Schinkel converted this former manor house into a
classical château in the style of a Roman country house.
Château Klein-Glienicke is surrounded by a 250-acre landscape
park laid out by Peter Lenne.*

75

„Schräge" Berlin-Tipps

Hangar II

Im Flughafen Tempelhof, Einfahrt Columbiadamm.
Sonnabends ab 23 Uhr
(zweimal im Monat!)
Die Kenner des Berliner Nachtlebens (und
solche, die es werden wollen) treffen sich alle
14 Tage im Berliner Flughafen Tempelhof.
Die Kulisse ist beeindruckend, Platz gibt es
genug, und laut darf es auch sein. In Anleh-
nung an den legendären Hangar in der schotti-
schen Stadt Ayr feiert man die Party nur einige
Nummern größer mit House-Music, aufgelegt
von internationalen Star-DJs.

Tanztee bei bebop

Gneisenaustraße 109, Gewerbehof Aufgang III
10961 Berlin
Telefon: 030 / 694 11 01
Sonntags 19–22 Uhr
Die Berliner Tanzszene findet sich jeden Sonn-
tag in der Tanzschule bebop zusammen, um
bei einer besonderen, manches Mal jazzigen
Musikmischung ihrer Leidenschaft zu frönen,
gleich ob sie aus dem Lager des Rumba, Tango
oder ChaChaCha ursprünglich kommt.

Friedrichstadtpalast

Friedrichstraße 107
10117 Berlin
Telefon: 030 / 23 26 20
Die schönsten und langbeinigsten Damen
zeigen hier in professionellen Revuen ihre tänze-
rische Perfektion. Gelegentlich stehen auch
buntdrollige Kinderrevuen auf dem Programm.

Velotaxi

Telefon: 030 / 44 35 89 91
Telefax: 030 / 44 35 89 99
Vorbestellung: 0172 / 31 36 655
Bis 2001 werden 60 Fahrradtaxen im Linien-
und Taxibetrieb der Hauptstadt eingesetzt
sein. Mit Velotaxi sind drei Linien befahrbar:
Tiergarten (Zoologischer Garten, durch den
Tiergarten zum Brandenburger Tor),
Kurfürstendamm (Adenauerplatz zum Witten-
bergplatz) und „Unter den Linden"(vom
Brandenburger Tor zum Alexanderplatz). Auch
Hochzeitspaare können auf diesen umwelt-
freundlichen Taxiservice zurückgreifen und sich
in weißen Velos durch die Stadt radeln lassen.

Broker's Bier Börse

Schiffbauerdamm 8
10117 Berlin
Telefon: 030 / 30 87 22 93
Alle Getränke sind an dieser Börse notiert.
Die Nachfrage bestimmt wie immer den Preis.
Ein unbedingtes Angebot für erfahrene
Spekulanten und solche, die es werden wollen.
Frühstück ab 9 Uhr.

Tränenpalast

Am Bahnhof Friedrichstraße
10117 Berlin
Telefon: 030 / 23 86 211
Millionen Ein -und Ausreisende haben diese
Halle passiert, in der einst die Grenzformali-
täten stattfanden. Heute werden hier Kabarett,
Jazz, Salsa, Modenschauen und Promi-Partys
veranstaltet.

Verkehrsberuhigte Ostzone (VEB)

Auguststraße 92
10117 Berlin
Telefon: 030 / 28 39 14 40
Man findet alles wieder: Stammtischwimpel
der Betriebskampfgruppe, FDJ-Fähnchen,
SED-Abzeichen oder die Lettern von Konsum
oder HO. Im ostalgischen Schankkeller werden
die Gäste platziert auf Gestühl in Form von
halben Trabis, und die abgeschabten Wände
erzählen ihre eigene Geschichte. Spaß ist dennoch oder vielleicht gerade darum garantiert.

Hackesche Höfe

Rosenthaler, Ecke Oranienburger Straße
10117 Berlin
Benannt nach einem Berliner Stadtkommandanten aus der Mitte des 18. Jahrhunderts,
gelten die Höfe nach ihrer mustergültigen
Sanierung als eines der größten europäischen
Wohn- und Gewerbehof-Ensembles.
Die Jugendstil-Anlage überstand die Kriege des
20. Jahrhunderts unbeschädigt, verrottete zur
DDR-Zeit, war aber der Augapfel des Denk-
malschutzes, der den Abriss verhinderte.
Der Hofkomplex wurde restauriert nach dem
Motto: Alte Substanz erhalten, aber mit fri-
schem Inhalt füllen. Diese Mischung ist gelun-
gen. Es gibt viele Lokale und Ladenzeilen, und
in der warmen Jahreszeit trifft man sich in den
Höfen wie auf einer italienischen Piazza.

Ständige Vertretung

Schiffbauerdamm 8
10117 Berlin
Telefon: 030 / 282 39 65
In Bonn gab es einen Aufschrei, als zwei städt-
chenberühmte Traditionswirte, die vehement
gegen Berlin als Hauptstadt protestiert hatten,
nach der Niederlage Bonns bei der Abstimmung
im Deutschen Bundestag erklärten, nun würden
auch sie nach Berlin ziehen. Ihre „StäV", wie
Insider kürzeln, ist inzwischen ein Sammel-
punkt der rheinischen Klientel an Bundestags-
abgeordneten und eines der originellsten Lokale
Berlins. Das „Gaffel Kölsch" fließt in Strömen,
und es gibt „Flamekuchen" wie am Rhein.

Hofbarbier

Eisenacher Straße 115
10777 Berlin
Telefon 030 / 215 91 14
Haupthaare in einer Vollmondnacht
geschnitten wachsen schneller, werden länger
und kräftiger. Mondphasen haben Einfluss auf
unseren Körper – so sagt man. Umgesetzt wird
diese Erkenntnis alle 2-3 Monate bei
der Haarschneide-Party mit Live-Musik im
Hofbarbier.

Bochardt

Französische Straße 47
10117 Berlin
Zu Kaisers Zeiten war dieses Restaurant welt-
berühmt. Heute ist es wieder ein beliebter
Treffpunkt am Gendarmenmarkt. Eine hohe
Halle mit Mosaiken, Fußböden aus der
wilhelminischen Zeit und am Abend reichlich
Prominenz.

Filmbühne am Steinplatz

Hardenbergstraße 12
10623 Berlin-Charlottenburg
Telefon: 030 / 31 26 589
Eines der ältesten Kinos Deutschlands mit Café
und Restaurant.

Clärchens Ballhaus

Auguststraße 24, 10117 Berlin
Es ist wie in alten Zeiten: Zille-Zeichnungen an
den Wänden, auf der Bühne spielt eine Band
live alte Schlager. Clärchens Ballhaus ist ein
Tanzlokal im traditionellen Stil.

Alternative places to go in Berlin

Hangar II
Tempelhof Airport, entrance Columbiadamm.
Saturdays: 11pm (only twice a month)
Experts of Berlin's nightlife (including budding ones) meet at Berlin's Tempelhof Airport every 14 days. The setting is amazing, there's enough space for everyone, and loud isn't the word for it! Inspired by the legendary Hangar in the Scottish town of Ayr, it's party time on an unparalleled scale with house music presented by international star DJs.

Thé dansant at bebop's
Gneisenaustrasse 109, arcade – stairway III
10961 Berlin
Tel. +49 (0) 30 694 1101
Sundays 7–10pm
Berlin's dancing fans meet every Sunday at bebop's dancing school to indulge their passion for the rumba, tango and cha-cha-cha to a very special (sometimes jazzy) musical mix.

Friedrichstadtpalast
Friedrichstrasse 107
10117 Berlin
Tel. +49 (0) 30 232620
Revue theatre featuring the classiest ladies with the longest legs and the best dancing feet in town. Cute children's shows are also sometimes on the bill.

Velotaxi
Tel. +49 (0) 30 4435 8991
Fax. +49 (0) 30 4435 8999
Bookings: +49 (0) 172 313 6655
By 2001, 60 eco-friendly bicycle taxis will be operating in the capital, some running regular services. Three lines are currently served by velotaxi: Tiergarten (Zoological Garden, via Tiergarten to the Brandenburg Gate), Kurfürstendamm (Adenauerplatz to Wittenbergplatz) and Unter den Linden (from the Brandenburg Gate to Alexanderplatz). White velotaxis make a great way for wedding couples to ride through Berlin.

„Mobilität dank Muskelkraft". Mit den Velotaxi von April bis Oktober durch Berlin.

"Muscle-power mobility." You can travel through Berlin by bicycle taxi between April and October.

Broker's Bier Börse
Schiffbauerdamm 8
10117 Berlin
Tel. +49 (0) 030 3087 2293
This bar functions like a stock exchange, with all drinks being listed commodities. Price depends on demand. A must for those with or seeking money-market experience. Breakfast from 9am.

Tränenpalast ("Palace of Tears")
At Friedrichstrasse Station
10117 Berlin
Tel. +49 (0) 30 238 6211
Millions of those entering and leaving East Berlin passed through this hall which used to house one of the busiest checkpoints. Nowadays it's a venue for cabaret, jazz, salsa, fashion shows and celebrity parties.

Verkehrsberuhigte Ostzone (VEB)
Auguststrasse 92
10117 Berlin
Tel. +49 (0) 30 2839 1440
The place to go for a little 'ostalgia' – Free German Youth flags and Party badges, seating made out of Trabant cars and the shabby walls all have their own story to tell. You're in for a fun time here – but we're not sure if that's because of or in spite of the atmosphere!

Filmbühne am Steinplatz
Hardenbergstrasse 12
10623 Berlin-Charlottenburg
Tel. +49 (0) 30 312 6589
One of Germany's oldest cinemas with a café and restaurant. Breakfast from 9am, films shown daily from 5pm.

Hackesche Höfe
Rosenthaler Strasse/juction
Oranienburger Strasse
10117 Berlin
Named after a commandant of Berlin in the mid-18th century, following first-rate refurbishment Hackesche Höfe is now one of the largest European combined housing and business complexes. Reconstruction took place with the idea of breathing new life into historical buildings. In the summer, this successful blend of pubs, shops and attic flats has all the atmosphere of an Italian piazza.

Ständige Vertretung
Schiffbauerdamm 8
10117 Berlin
Tel. +49 (0) 30 282 3965
In Bonn there was an outcry when two landlords who vehemently protested against making Berlin the new capital also decided to move here after Bonn was defeated in the vote in the German parliament. Known as the "Ständige Vertretung" ("Permanent Representation" – the name used for West Germany's embassy in East Berlin), it has now become the place to meet for their MP clientele from the Rhine – and one of the most original pubs in Berlin. Gaffel Kölsch beer flows freely, and it's the place to sample that Rhine delicacy "Flamekuchen".

Hofbarbier
Eisenacher Strasse 115
10777 Berlin
Tel. +49 (0) 030 215 9114
Hair cut during a full moon grows quicker, longer and stronger. The phases of the moon are said to have an influence on the body. This idea is put to the test every 2–3 months at the haircutting party with live music hosted by Hofbarbier. Why waste the night by sleeping through it?

Clärchens Ballhaus
Auguststraße 24
10117 Berlin
It is just as in the old days: Drawings by the German artist Zille adorn the walls, on the stage a band plays live old hits.
Clärchens Ballhaus is a small dance hall in traditional style.

Brandenburg

Schmachtenhagen · Stolzenhagen · Lanke · Biesenthal

Oranienburg · Wandlitz · Grüntal

Brandenburg · Rüdnitz · Tempelfelde

Schwante · Zühlsdorf · Basdorf · Schönfeld

Leegebruch · Birkenwerder · Schönow · Bernau · Wilmersdorf

Velten · Hohen Neudorf · Buch · Zepernick · Werneuchen · Löhme

Marwitz · Bötzow · Frohnau · **Berlin** · **Brandenburg**

Wansdorf · Hennings-dorf · Hermsdorf · Lindenberg · Blumberg

Schönwalde · Heiligensee · Waldmanns-lust · Niederschön-hausen · Blanken-burg · Altlands-berg

Falkensee · Wittenau · Pankow · Weißensee · Marzahn · Hörnow · Neuenhagen

Spandau · Berlin-Tegel · Reinickendorf · SPREE QUELL · Hohen-schön-hausen · Hellersdorf

Dalgow-Döberitz · Wedding · Prenzlauer Berg · Lichtenberg · Mahlsdorf · Dahlwitz-Hoppegarten

Staaken · Schloß Charlotten-burg · Tiergarten · Mitte · Reichstag Brandenb. Tor · Friedrichshain · Friedrichs-felde · Kaulsdorf

Charlottenburg · Messegelände · Straße des 17. Juni · Leipziger Str. · Kreuzberg · Tierpark Berlin · Schöneiche

Gatow · Gedächtnis-kirche · Wilmers-dorf · Schöne-berg · Neukölln · Karlshorst · Treptow · Köpenick

Grune-wald · Schmargendorf · Berlin-Tempelhof · Ober-schönweide · Friedrichs-hagen · Rahnsdorf

Gr.-Glienicke · Dahlem · Tempelhof · Nieder-schönweide · Johannis-tal · Adlers-hof · Großer Müggelsee

Großer Wann-see · Unter den Eichen · Steglitz · Marien-dorf · Rudow · Langer See · Müggelheim

Wannsee · Zehlendorf · Lankwitz · Buckow · Alt-Glienicke · Bohns-dorf · Seddin-see

Potsdam · Lichter-felde · Marien-felde · Großziethen · Berlin-Schönefeld

Babelsberg · Kleinmachnow · Schönefeld · Eichenwalde · Werns-dorf

Drewitz · Teltow · Lichten-rade · Schulzen-dorf · Zeuthen

Stahnsdorf · Güterfelde · Großbeeren · Mahlow · Wildau

Bergholz-Rehbrücke · Blanken-felde · Dahlewitz · Zernsdorf

Wilhelmshorst · Rangsdorf · **Königs Wusterhausen** · Senzig

Ludwigsfelde · **Brandenburg** · Mittenwalde · Bestensee

© KARTOGRAPHIE Peh & Schefcik, Eppelheim

0   5 km

78

Literaturhinweise, Bildnachweis, Museen

Museen

Staatliche Museen zu Berlin
Info-Telefon: 030/20 90 55 55
Telefax: 030/20 90 55 02

Altes Museum
Bodestraße 1–3 (Eingang Lustgarten)
10178 Berlin

Pergamonmuseum
Bodestraße 1–3 (Eingang Kupfergraben)
10178 Berlin

Museum für Vor- und Frühgeschichte
Schloß Charlottenburg, Langhansbau
14059 Berlin

Sammlung Berggruen
Schloßstrasse 1
14059 Berlin

Gemäldegalerie
Kulturforum im Tiergarten
Matthäikirchplatz 8
10785 Berlin

Kunstgewerbemuseum
Matthäikirchplatz
10785 Berlin

Neue Nationalgalerie
Potsdamer Straße 50
10785 Berlin

Ägyptisches Museum und Papyrussammlung
Schloßstraße 70
14059 Berlin

Berliner Dom
Am Lustgarten
Telefon: 030/20 26 90

Brecht-Weigel-Gedenkstätte
Chausseestraße 125
10115 Berlin
Telefon: 030/2 83 05 70 44
Telefax: 030/2 83 05 70 33

Neue Synagoge Berlin – Centrum Judaicum
Oranienburger Straße 28–30
10117 Berlin
Telefon: 030/88 02 83 00
Telefax: 030/282 11 76

Deutsche Guggenheim Berlin
Unter den Linden 13–15
10117 Berlin
Telefon: 030/20 20 93-0
Telefax: 030/20 20 93-20

Hugenottenmuseum
Gendarmenmarkt 5
10117 Berlin
Telefon: 030/229 17 60
Telefax: 030/204 15 05

Märkisches Museum
Am Köllnischen Park 5
10179 Berlin
Telefon: 030/30 86 60
Telefax: 030/30 86 62 01

Museum für Naturkunde
Invalidenstraße 43
10115 Berlin
Telefon: 030/20 93 85 91
Telefax: 030/20 93 88 14

Ägyptisches Museum und Papyrussammlung
Schloßstraße 70
14059 Berlin

Bröhan-Museum
Schloßstraße 1a
14059 Berlin
Telefon: 030/32 69 06 00
Telefax: 030/32 69 06 26

Gedenkstätte Plötzensee
Hüttigpfad
13627 Berlin
Telefon: 030/344 32 26

Schloß Charlottenburg
Luisenplatz
14059 Berlin
Telefon: 030/32 09 11
Telefax: 030/32 09 12 00

Bauhaus-Archiv – Museum für Gestaltung
Klingelhöferstraße 14
10785 Berlin
Telefon: 030/254 00 20
Telefax: 030/25 40 02 10

Musikinstrumentenmuseum
Tiergartenstraße 1
10785 Berlin
Telefon: 030/25 48 11 78
Telefax: 030/25 48 11 72

Information

Berlin Tourismus Marketing GmbH
Am Karlsbad 11
10785 Berlin
Information: 0190/75 40 40
(DM 2,42/Min)
Reservierung: 030/25 00 25
Calls from abroad: + 49 1805-754040
Fax: 030/25 00 24 24
http://www.berlin-tourism.de
email: information@berlin-tourism

Der Autor

Moritz Fahrner, in Sachsen geboren, studierte Theologie und Germanistik in Berlin und ist heute als freier Journalist tätig. Als Autor zeichnet er für zahlreiche Reisebildbände und -führer verantwortlich.

Der Fotograf

Der Reise- und Städtefotograf Reiner Elsen lebt und arbeitet seit mehr als zwanzig Jahren in Berlin. Seine Arbeiten werden weltweit über ein Netz von Bildagenturen vertrieben. Schwerpunkt seiner Tätigkeit sind Fotos seiner Wahlheimat Berlin.

Bildnachweis

Reiner Elsen: Frontispiz, S. 5, 10, 11, 12, 14/15, 16 oben, 17, 18, 20, 22, 23, 27, 28, 30, 32, 33, 34, 35, 39, 42, 43, 44, 45, 49, 50, 52, 53 unten, 54 oben, 57 oben, 59 unten, 60, 61 oben, 62, 63, 66, 71 oben, 72 unten, 73 oben, 77
Erhard Pansegrau: S. 6, kleine Abb. im Titel
NBL-Bildarchiv: S. 7, 16 unten, 26, 36, 40, 46, 53 oben, 54 unten, 55, 57 unten, 58, 59 oben, 64/65, 72 oben
Ulf Böttcher: S. 24, 25 oben, 71 unten, 74, 75
Soenne Aachen: S. 56
Christiane v. Enzberg: S. 61 unten
Frank Ihlow: S. 70, 73 unten
Kartographie Peh & Schefcik: S. 78

Literaturhinweise

Ingrid Nowel, Vom preußischen Zentrum zur Neuen Hauptstadt
DuMont Kunstreiseführer, Köln 1998
Kristine Jaath, Hauptstadt Berlin
Reise KNOW-HOW Verlag Peter Rump, 1999
Berlin, ©Mairs Geographischer Verlag, 2000